UNEXPLAINED MYSTERIES OF HEAVEN AND EARTH

RON PHILLIPS, DMin

CHARISMA HOUSE

Most Charisma House Book Group products are available at special quantity discounts for bulk purchase for sales promotions, premiums, fund-raising, and educational needs. For details, write Charisma House Book Group, 600 Rinehart Road, Lake Mary, Florida 32746, or telephone (407) 333-0600.

Unexplained Mysteries of Heaven and Earth by Ron Phillips
Published by Charisma House
Charisma Media/Charisma House Book Group
600 Rinehart Road
Lake Mary, Florida 32746
www.charismahouse.com

Cover design by Lisa Rae Cox
Design Director: Bill Johnson

Visit the author's website at www.ronphillips.org.

Library of Congress Cataloging-in-Publication Data:
An application to register this book for cataloging has been submitted to the Library of Congress.
International Standard Book Number: 978-1-62136-253-1

E-book ISBN: 978-1-62136-254-8

While the author has made every effort to provide accurate telephone numbers and Internet addresses at the time of publication, neither the publisher nor the author assumes any responsibility for errors or for changes that occur after publication.

First edition

13 14 15 16 17 — 9 8 7 6 5 4 3 2 1
Printed in the United States of America

CONTENTS

ACKNOWLEDGMENTS

I WANT TO THANK James Marler for his exhaustive and extensive help in the first draft of this book. Also I want to thank Bill Fry at anchorstone.com for permission to explain the very thorough research of the late Ron Wyatt for chapters 4, 8, and 9. I appreciate Bill's frank approach to the purported uncovering of the ark of the covenant. This information is controversial and challenged by many. I make no claim to its authenticity. In a mystery book there will always be disagreement over the unknown.

A big thank-you to the members of Abba's House and to the staff and partners of Ron Phillips Ministries. Also, a big thanks is due to Andrea Ridge for her able assistance in all of my ministries.

A final thank-you to Jevon Bolden and all the great staff at Charisma House.

PROLOGUE

WHILE WE ARE grateful for the witness of Holy Scriptures and the cry of our own conscience as witness to our God and Savior, there are other witnesses. The Scripture clearly indicates that the creative order itself cries out as a witness to God. Psalm 19:1 says that "the heavens declare the glory of God; and the firmament shows His handiwork."

The vast reaches of outer space and its unending marvel cry out to the glory of God. Radio telescopes are picking up sounds from beyond our galaxy. The whole of creation is a divine symphony. Furthermore, Scripture says that "truth shall spring out of the earth" (Ps. 85:11). The vast and unexplained mystery of the earth cries out for our inspection and study.

The Discovery Channel, the National Geographic Channel, the History Channel, and others are exploring the vast and unanswered mysteries of our earth. Their programs garner vast audiences. More than one half of their shows have to do with historical, archaeological, and scientific mysteries related to our Bible.

For that reason I do not shrink from probing some of their mysteries. I do not declare my research to be infallible, and much of it, though drawn from reliable sources, is my own interpretation. I do believe the scriptures that order us to study these mysteries:

> The works of the LORD are great, studied by all who have pleasure in them.
> —PSALM 111:2

We should not be afraid to view with wonder the ancient works of our Lord:

> For You, Lord, have made me glad through Your work; I will triumph in the works of Your hands. O Lord, how great are Your works! Your thoughts are very deep. A senseless man does not know, nor does a fool understand this.
>
> —Psalm 92:4–6

Like David, I love to study the ancient things God has marked for us on this earth:

> I remember the days of old; I meditate on all Your works; I muse on the work of Your hands. I spread out my hands to You; my soul longs for You like a thirsty land.
>
> —Psalm 143:5–6

Indeed, in these last days we do well to explore the mysteries of God and to behold in wonder His greatness. The vast size and scope of the ever-expanding creation alone should cause us to bow in worship and wonder.

Our pride and arrogance can be broken as we explore the secrets of old and discover that with God there is really "nothing new under the sun" (Eccles. 1:9).

We know that the mysteries of heaven and earth can be revealed to those who are baptized in the Holy Spirit. The Holy Spirit is our guarantee of the mysteries of heaven until we arrive there. Ephesians 1:14 says that the Holy Spirit "is the guarantee of our inheritance until the redemption of the purchased possession, to the praise of His glory."

In the meantime as spiritual beings we can receive the things that are of God! We can receive revelation or enlightenment from God to understand His created order.

> [May] the God of our Lord Jesus Christ, the Father of glory…give to you the spirit of wisdom and revelation in the knowledge of Him, the eyes of your understanding being enlightened; that you may know what is the hope of His

calling, what are the riches of the glory of His inheritance in the saints.
—EPHESIANS 1:17–18

God will open our eyes to His truth and give us revelation of His power in all of His works. God continues to unfold truth today, not simply with Scripture, but truth that opens the blinded eyes of the lost. We must be firmly grounded in "present truths."

For this reason I will not be negligent to remind you always of these things, though you know and are established in the present truth.
—2 PETER 1:12

TRUTH SPRINGS

In Psalm 85:11 David wrote the following:

Truth shall spring out of the earth, and righteousness shall look down from heaven.

This verse, probably more than any other, lit the fire under me to look to the signs in the earth that speak to the truth of God, the Bible, and the gospel of Jesus Christ. However, it was pondering these words of David in combination with the words of John, the beloved apostle, that solidified my certainty that I share these mysteries. I will refer to these verses throughout this book, but let me lay a foundation first.

In 1 John 5:6–8 we read:

This is He who came by water and blood—Jesus Christ; not only by water, but by water and blood. And it is the Spirit who bears witness, because the Spirit is truth. For there are three that bear witness in heaven: the Father, the Word, and the Holy Spirit; and these three are one. And there are three that bear witness on earth: the Spirit, the water, and the blood; and these three agree as one.

So many people think that Christianity is simply a "fairy tale" religion complete with talking snakes and donkeys, magical fruit and water, seer mystics and paranormal healings, but it is simply not so. Christianity is a religion founded on fact. Yes, the Bible says that we have witnesses for the truth of our salvation in heaven. John says that the Father, the Son, and the Holy Spirit—the three yet one—bear witness of our salvation in heaven. Moreover, and more importantly for our purposes here, John says that there are on the earth, right now at this moment, other witnesses. Specifically the Spirit, the water, and the blood attest to the truth. That says to me that there is physical evidence on this planet to the truth of Scripture.

Perhaps this evidence has been lost in legend and lore. Often I have been confronted by people bringing up some of the very mysteries we will discuss in this book as evidence that Christianity cannot possibly be true. I believe it is important for believers to equip themselves with at least cursory information about these things so that we can be prepared, should the opportunity arise, to discuss these issues.

Therefore we will explore the mysteries of the Bible: historical, scientific, practical, and theological. Those of us who speak in tongues know that we speak "mysteries" (1 Corinthians 14:2—"For he who speaks in a tongue does not speak to men but to God, for no one understands him; however, in the spirit he speaks mysteries.")

Both the Hebrew word *raz* and the Greek word *musterion*, which are translated "mystery," mean "something real that is hidden." There is real history we do not know. There is a loving God whom we can know. There are insights we can gain! This writing desires to cause those who read it to catch their breath in wonder and worship before God. Our goal is not to hear them say "Amen" but "Wow! God is great."

So join me as we travel back beyond time, as we look at the Flood, lost Atlantis, the Great Pyramid of Giza, the ark of the covenant, Melchizedek, Sodom and Gomorrah, the giants, Christ, the Antichrist, the Rapture, spiritual fullness, and other mysteries!

You will say at times, "I did not know that!" More than learn facts, may you come to know the truth of God and the God of truth more!

Chapter 1

The MYSTERY *of the* ORIGINAL EARTH

O NE OF THE greatest mysteries of history is how the earth could be old and yet Adam's race less than ten thousand years old! Today there is much disagreement among Christians as to whether the earth is young or old. There is a theory called the gap theory that is biblically consistent with our ancient original earth and a young human race.

According to this view, a pristine and beautiful world existed in the ancient past. This prehistorical world was created by the Word of God: "In the beginning God created the heavens and the earth" (Gen. 1:1).

Our universe with all its galaxies, solar systems, and vast expanses of space, size, and mysteries was created before our time. Science declares that our universe is still expanding, stars exploding and imploding, and even solar systems being birthed.

The Scriptures speak of this ancient world. In 2 Peter 3:5–7 we are told:

> For this they willfully forget: that by the word of God the heavens were of old, and the earth standing out of water and in the water, by which the world that then existed perished, being flooded with water. But the heavens and the earth which are now preserved by the same word, are reserved for fire until the day of judgment and perdition of ungodly men.

Notice the phrase "the heavens were of old." Obviously our Lord, who is called "the Ancient of Days," had in the distant past set all of this in motion. A destroyed solar system had left the earth flooded completely—so much so that it looked like a cork bobbing in the water. The text says, "The world that then existed perished."

This is not Noah's flood but a worse catastrophe! Remember that in Genesis 1:2 we are told that "the earth was *without form, and void*; and darkness was on the face of the deep. And the Spirit of God was hovering over the face of the waters" (emphasis added).

This can be translated, "The earth became without form and void." Between the first two verses of Genesis, there was a horrific, cataclysmic event that totally destroyed an ancient inhabited world.

The passage in 2 Peter 3 indicates a complete destruction of the world. This is not the flood of Noah. We are still living on the same world of Noah's flood.

Genesis 1:2 indicates a flooded world, a dark world whose source of light was gone. Undoubtedly the entire planet and its ancient solar system were destroyed in a cosmic event beyond our understanding.

THE PRE-ADAMIC WORLD

You see, "the world that then existed" describes a world that has left some footprints on this present world. I agree with Gaines Johnson in his excellent book *The Bible Genesis & Geology* that the Bible clearly teaches plural earths. "These are the generations of the heavens and of the earth when they were created, in the day that the LORD God made earth and heaven" (Gen. 2:4, KJV).

The word *generations* is plural, indicating two creative events. The earth has an old history that is a mystery and a more recent history of humankind.

What happened between Genesis 1:1 and 1:2 rendered the earth "without form and void." Isaiah supports the gap theory by declaring that God did not create the old earth "in vain," or *tohuw*. The earth became *tohuw* according to Genesis 1:2.

Now this empty, dark, flooded earth was devoid of any life forms.

When God said, "Let there be light," the flooded, ruined earth was already here! An ancient world full of animal life was gone.

What happened to the old earth?

There are a few glimpses of this old world. Some of course are written in nature: the vast geologic strata, the fossils, the dinosaurs, and carbon-based energy sources. All of geology and archeology seem to point to a very old world.

There is, however, one clear biblical glimpse of that world. Ezekiel 28 records a world in which Lucifer ruled and led worship. Also the prophet Isaiah speaks of a horrific fall by Lucifer that wrought destruction. Let me share the following explanations of this mystery.

First, Lucifer was originally a beautiful creature reflecting the glory of God. Ezekiel 28:12 says:

> Son of man, take up a lamentation for the king of Tyre, and say to him, "Thus says the Lord GOD: 'You were the seal of perfection, full of wisdom and perfect in beauty.'"

Second, he ruled over the earth from a land called Eden, which I believe was the capital of the old world. In that place Lucifer reflected from his jewel-covered body the light of God's glory. He also led praise and worship for all the inhabitants of the earth, which included a vast population of angels. Lucifer carried the anointing of God and was assigned to be a protective covering for the angelic world. Ezekiel goes on to say in verses 13–14:

> You were in Eden, the garden of God; every precious stone was your covering: the sardius, topaz, and diamond, beryl, onyx, and jasper, sapphire, turquoise, and emerald with gold. The workmanship of your timbrels and pipes was prepared for you on the day you were created.
>
> You were the anointed cherub who covers; I established

you; you were on the holy mountain of God; you walked back
and forth in the midst of fiery stones.

This text indicates that Lucifer is a created being called a cherub!
The cherubim are the four-faced creatures found in the early chapters of Ezekiel and in Revelation 4. The number *four* is the number
of the earth. Lucifer's assignment was to steward this planet for
God's purposes.

Lucifer knew the secrets of unlimited power for this planet.
As we just saw, Ezekiel 28:14 says of him, "You were the anointed
cherub who covers; I established you; you were on the holy mountain of God; you walked back and forth in the midst of fiery stones."
I believe the stones of fire were the energy source for the ancient
world. These stones supplied light, heat, and energy to the old earth.
Here is a picture of a planet full of animal life mingling with the
angels and exploding in praise to its Creator!

Then tragedy struck! Lucifer tried to breach the heavenly dimension and seize the throne of God with one third of the angels! The
result was a tremendous fall. Ezekiel 28:16–17 says:

> By the abundance of your trading you became filled with vio-
> lence within, and you sinned; therefore I cast you as a profane
> thing out of the mountain of God; and I destroyed you, O
> covering cherub, from the midst of the fiery stones.
>
> Your heart was lifted up because of your beauty; you cor-
> rupted your wisdom for the sake of your splendor; I cast you
> to the ground, I laid you before kings, that they might gaze
> at you.

Isaiah gives us a more detailed explanation of what transpired
in Isaiah 14:13–14:

> For you have said in your heart: "I will ascend into heaven,
> I will exalt my throne above the stars of God; I will also sit
> on the mount of the congregation on the farthest sides of the

north; I will ascend above the heights of the clouds, I will be like the Most High."

Notice the use of the phrase "I will" by Lucifer. He gives up his clear goal by saying, "I will be like the Most High."

This decision led to a cosmic catastrophe that brought cataclysmic repercussion to the old earth. Lucifer's fall was like an asteroid hitting the planet. All of prehistoric life was destroyed. This fall was of monumental proportions. The earth became without form and void! (For more information see my book *Everyone's Guide to Demons and Spiritual Warfare*.)

ENTER ADAM

Between six and ten thousand years ago God returns to the ruined planet and sets it aright. He releases energy, resets the orbits around the sun. He moves some of the water off the earth. (Could it be the crystal sea at the border of the heavenly dimensions? See Revelation 4:6.)

God then visits that area called Eden in the ancient world. There God sets a garden in the midst of that vast land of four rivers. Lurking in that garden is the former cherub that has become a monster, Lucifer, now Satan.

That is the mystery of how an old earth and a young Adam are possible. Even Satan's fall was used to prepare energy resources that we still use today! Also DNA evidence shows only a tiny connection between humans today and the humanlike fossil of so-called ancient man (one part in a million for Cro-Magnon).

There were creations, no doubt, of many kind in the old earth. Yet only six thousand years ago God set us here in His image!

THE MYSTERY REVEALED

The real mystery of the old earth is that we do not know much concretely about it. But what we can know of it surprises us about this earth. God created this earth for us. It is a special place that was meant to be a kind of "home base" for God's creation. Because of the fall it has been corrupted, but just as God re-formed the old earth and created the one we now know, He will once again make a new heaven and a new earth where we can live with Him, in the state He intended for us to live in Eden, forever.

Chapter 2

The MYSTERY *of the* DAYS *of* NOAH

I

T IS DISMISSED by skeptics as absurd. It is constantly referred to as a corruption of the Epic of Gilgamesh. The global Flood is a story that exists in over six hundred cultures that we know of. Sociologists and anthropologists tell us that the more often we see a legend or myth in disparate cultures, the greater the probability that the story has truth in history. Jesus said that the "days of Noah" would be a sign to us (Luke 17:26). It is important then for us to understand as much as we can about the world in which Noah found himself—a world so depraved that God determined that the only hope for humanity was to wipe people out almost completely and start again. What was that world like?

CHARACTERISTICS OF THE DAYS OF NOAH

In Noah's day there was a rapid increase in population. This was partly due to the amount of time that people lived. Noah's age at the time of the Flood was a staggering 600 years old. He lived until he was 950. Each calendar year affords the opportunity for at least one live birth. When Noah began building the ark, this world had existed for at least 1,600 years. What this tells us is that if a life span was an average of 400 years, and a family had only six children, then we can estimate the population of the pre-Flood world at around seven billion people. Sociologically speaking, the greater number of people in the populace, the more accelerated the evil.

Additionally we know that in Noah's day there had been great advances in technology and civilization. Cain taught the people to settle in cities as opposed to living a Bedouin type of lifestyle. "And Cain knew his wife, and she conceived and bore Enoch. And he built a city, and called the name of the city after the name of his son—Enoch" (Gen. 4:17).

Mechanical and fine arts were introduced in an effort to overcome the curse of labor. We only have some vague hints as to the civilization, art, and inventions of the pre-Flood people.

Just a few generations after Cain, we read about Jabal, who led a revolution of animal husbandry (Gen. 4:20), his brother Jubal, who is called the "father of all those who play the harp and flute" (Gen. 4:21), and their brother Tubal-Cain, who instructed in the craft of bronze and iron (Gen. 4:22).

Pre-Flood wonders

The Great Pyramid at Giza (which will be discussed in chapter 3) is believed by many to have been built prior to the Flood and was renovated and expanded by Pharaoh Khufu. They point to its structure (built on solid bedrock), to its setting, and to science.

The Assyrian library of Agade was established by the Akkadian king Sargon in Uruk, called "the city of books."[1] As early as 2650 BC the library existed with ancient books, tablets, scrolls, and art. According to the ancient historian Berossus, it was here that Noah buried in waterproof containers the contents of the ancient library and disentombed it after the Flood.[2]

CORRUPTION IN THE DAYS OF NOAH

I mentioned the population explosion in the previous section. An important aspect of this is that the population was not exploding with just humans. Genesis 6:1–2 tells us:

> Now it came to pass, when men began to multiply on the face of the earth, and daughters were born to them, that the sons of God saw the daughters of men, that they were beautiful; and they took wives for themselves of all whom they chose.

Here we have the intermarriage of the descendants of Cain and Seth with embodied demons. This produced a race of people called "giants" by the English Bible. They are literally *Nephilim*, which means "fallen ones." They occupied the land of Canaan. (This view is supported by Flavius Josephus[3] and Philo Judaeus.[4]) These beings produced a subhuman or hybrid race prior to the Flood. These hybrid beings could be the beings that became the ancient mythological gods. (See John Fleming's *The Fallen Angel and the Heroes of Mythology* and Thomas Horn's *Nephilim Stargates*). This race brought vile immorality, crime, terror, and war to the earth. For our day it could mean a new influx of demonic influence. We have a grievous picture of what this means in Numbers 13:32–33:

> And they gave the children of Israel a bad report of the land which they had spied out, saying, "The land through which we have gone as spies is a land that devours its inhabitants, and all the people whom we saw in it are men of great stature. There we saw the giants (the descendants of Anak came from the giants); and we were like grasshoppers in our own sight, and so we were in their sight."

As we can see, these hybrids were present when the children of Israel entered the land of promise.

David would finally wipe them out (we assume). The human race seems to have experienced this activity before the Flood and in seizing Canaan during the Exodus. In the last days this pit will be opened, and the Antichrist will be the seed of Satan born to a woman.

The Nephilim

These fallen angels, Nephilim, left their own estate and cohabitated with women and produced horror for the earth. These demons disrupted God's order on earth. This is why the Flood came. It explains the order by God to kill the inhabitants of Canaan. Many of them were not fully human.

For the sake of clarity it needs to be explained that while this initial population of Nephilim were eliminated by the Flood, the abomination happened again. In Genesis 6:4 we read:

> There were giants on the earth in those days, *and also afterward*, when the sons of God came in to the daughters of men and they bore children to them. Those were the mighty men who were of old, men of renown.
>
> —EMPHASIS ADDED

This indicates that after the Flood these fallen angels came again and procreated with the "daughters of men." But is it just a "story" from the Bible? Could it have really happened?

The wonderful aspect of this is that God's Word is true, and truth does indeed "spring from the earth." The Nephilim are, as some have said, the "elephant in the room" for the archeological, anthropological, and scientific communities. Here are some interesting examples:

- In AD 1692 a skeleton was found near Angers, France, of a man measuring seventeen feet, four inches.[5]

- In 1950 in the Euphrates Valley of Southeast Turkey several tombs were found containing full skeletons of giants fourteen to sixteen feet tall.[6]

- Digs in China have uncovered skeletal remains of giants over fifteen feet tall.[7]

But the evidence is not relegated to just skeletal remains.

- I once visited the Heraklion Archaeological Museum in Crete, and there exists an exhibit of ancient bronze battle-axes from as far back as 1700 BC. This is not that unusual until you consider that the axes are over five feet in length. These are not, as some assert, decorative, but show signs of use in battle.

- In the Great Orme Copper mine in the coastal town of Llandudno in North Wales, sledgehammers of over sixty pounds each have been found.[8] These hammers, used in the mining of copper, would have had handles of approximately nine feet.

How amazing it is that God's truth is today springing from the earth!

Callousness of Noah's day

During the century or so that it took Noah and his family to build the ark, Noah continually warned the people about the coming flood. But no one listened to Noah's warnings! There was a business-as-usual indifference to the word and to his construction project and its warning. Furthermore we know that Enoch preached and warned the people:

> Now Enoch, the seventh from Adam, prophesied about these men also, saying, "Behold, the Lord comes with ten thousands of His saints, to execute judgment on all, to convict all who are ungodly among them of all their ungodly deeds which they have committed in an ungodly way, and of all the harsh things which ungodly sinners have spoken against Him."
> —JUDE 14–15

The problem was not in the preaching or the warnings. The problem was not even in the truth. It was that the people of Noah's day could not be bothered to listen to the warnings.

WHAT'S IN A NAME?

I know parents who struggled over what to name their child, wanting that perfect balance of familial importance, syllabic rhythm, and name meaning. We see evidence in the Bible that the name we give our child has great significance. This is truer in Genesis than we might realize.

We see that Noah's lineage is clear. His father, Lamech, was the son of Methuselah (the oldest man who ever lived), who was the son of Enoch, who was the son of Jared, who was the son of Mahalalel, who was the son of Kenan (or Cainan), who was the son of Enosh, who was the son of Seth, who was the son of Adam (Gen. 5).

Now I know that sounds like the beginning of Matthew's Gospel, but I include these men to show you a wonderful hidden gospel. The name *Adam* comes from the Hebrew word that means "man." Adam's son Seth was an appointed replacement for the loss of both Cain and the murdered Abel. His name means "appointed." The name *Enosh* is somewhat tricky. It means both "woeful" and "wicked" but also "mortal." The name *Kenan* means "sorrow," while Kenan's son Mahalalel had a name meaning "the blessed God." The name *Jared* means "descent" or "one who will descend," while Jared's son Enoch had a name that meant "teaching" or "one who teaches."

Methuselah, who died the same year that the Flood happened, had a name that meant "his death shall bring (it)." Noah's father, Lamech, had a name meaning "despairing" or "one who despairs," while Noah's name meant "comfort" or "rest."

When we look at this line of men, we see a hidden gospel in the meanings of their names. When we look past the surface, we see that "man appointed woeful, wicked, mortal sorrow" (Adam, Seth, and Enosh). But "the blessed God shall come down teaching" (Mahalalel, Jared, and Enoch). And "his death shall bring those who despair comfort" (Methuselah, Lamech, and Noah). What a wonderful picture this is of our Lord and Savior!

THE MYSTERY REVEALED

In the past two centuries the growth of the world's population has been staggering. In AD 1800 world population estimates were at approximately one billion people. By 1900 the population had not yet reached two billion. However, starting in 1950, the number (then at two and a half billion) began a rapid increase. By 2000 the number sat at six billion, and in 2010 the number had increased to seven billion.[9] The UN growth estimates for the next century are overwhelming. On the low end, when accounting for disease and war, there could be a drop in population to just over six billion. The high-end probability is that the number could grow to over fifteen billion. The median expectation is that by 2100, the world population will be at ten billion people.[10]

The twentieth century has shown dramatic increases in technology. I am always amazed that there are people who do not know that a computer used to be the size of a small house. There is in computing circles "Moore's Law," which states that "processor speeds, or overall processing power for computers, will double every two years."[11] This, of course, affects computer-processing speeds, which affect the number of instructions per second (IPS, measured in thousands and millions) that the computer can perform.

In 1971 the Intel 4004 processor could perform only .092 MIPS. In 1982 the Intel 80286 processor could perform 2.66 MIPS. By 2011 the Intel Core i7-Extreme Edition 3960X processor could clock 177,730 MIPS. Let that sink in. That Intel Core processor could perform 177,730,000,000 instructions every second. Additionally computer storage spaces have increased dramatically in the past few decades. It is now possible to carry more information than is contained in a small library on a flash drive smaller than your thumb.

It is so easy to see what God meant when He said of the people gathered at the Tower of Babel, "Now nothing that they propose to do will be withheld from them" (Gen. 11:6). Knowledge is increasing very rapidly. Consider the prophecy given in Daniel:

At that time Michael shall stand up, the great prince who stands watch over the sons of your people; and there shall be a time of trouble, such as never was since there was a nation, even to that time. And at that time your people shall be delivered, every one who is found written in the book. And many of those who sleep in the dust of the earth shall awake, some to everlasting life, some to shame and everlasting contempt. Those who are wise shall shine like the brightness of the firmament, and those who turn many to righteousness like the stars forever and ever.

But you, Daniel, shut up the words, and seal the book until the time of the end; many shall run to and fro, and knowledge shall increase.

—Daniel 12:1–4

Jesus pointed to the "days of Noah" as a sign of the end times. Before He comes again, the Enoch generation will be raptured. The end-times Jewish generation will go through the Flood (or the time of Tribulation). In Luke 17:20–27 we see Jesus point to this:

Now when He was asked by the Pharisees when the kingdom of God would come, He answered them and said, "The kingdom of God does not come with observation; nor will they say, 'See here!' or 'See there!' For indeed, the kingdom of God is within you."

Then He said to the disciples, "The days will come when you will desire to see one of the days of the Son of Man, and you will not see it. And they will say to you, 'Look here!' or 'Look there!' Do not go after them or follow them. For as the lightning that flashes out of one part under heaven shines to the other part under heaven, so also the Son of Man will be in His day. But first He must suffer many things and be rejected by this generation. And as it was in the days of Noah, so it will be also in the days of the Son of Man: They ate, they drank, they married wives, they were given in marriage, until the day that Noah entered the ark, and the flood came and destroyed them all."

Do not be among those who do not see the signs of Jesus's coming. Noah preached to the lost of his day for over a century. Today the mystery is revealed to us so that no one will endure the flood without due warning and knowledge that Jesus has prepared a way for you, for me, for all of us to escape the coming flood of judgment.

Chapter 3

The MYSTERY *of the* GREAT PYRAMID

N EAR CAIRO RESTS the only one of the Seven Wonders of the Ancient World still standing: the Great Pyramid of Giza. This pyramid was the first and largest of twenty-three found in Giza Necropolis. Oddly enough ancient pyramidal structures are found all over the world.

I am convinced that this building is a sermon in stone left by the Lord as a witness to His divine existence, His greatness, His plan. The world of the Great Pyramid tradition says that Pharaoh Khufu built the pyramid, but subsequent scholarship has surmised that Khufu claimed the pyramid and then rebuilt or expanded it. In 1857 Auguste Mariette discovered a stele (a hieroglyphic stone with a story) wherein Khufu tells of his own discovery of the Great Pyramid. This stele says of Khufu, "He built again [the] temple of stone."[1] Khufu built the three small pyramids next to the Great Pyramid for his family.

There are countless theories regarding the actual building of the pyramid. Some say that "gods" or "aliens" from outer space came and built the pyramid. There are theories that say the pyramid must have been built in the antediluvian civilization. I am of the opinion that a biblical character was at least involved—possibly Seth but, again, in my opinion, probably Job—and guided by the hand of God.

Herodotus declared that a "noted stranger," who was also a shepherd, lived in Egypt at the time of Pharaoh Khufu and built the Pyramid of Giza. He is called "Philitis" by both Egyptian and

Greek historians. Josephus talks of "shepherd kings" who had Egypt "in their hands." These shepherd kings were known as Hyskos. They were the mighty Arabs of the past. Joseph Seiss, Bible scholar and historian, says that the Arab was Job. Seiss says that God addresses the image of the pyramid, comparing Job's construction with God's creation of the world.[2] In Job 38:2–7 we read:

> Who is this who darkens counsel by words without knowledge? Now prepare yourself like a man; I will question you, and you shall answer Me.
>
> Where were you when I laid the foundations of the earth? Tell Me, if you have understanding. Who determined its measurements? Surely you know! Or who stretched the line upon it? To what were its foundations fastened? Or who laid its cornerstone, when the morning stars sang together, and all the sons of God shouted for joy?

For this illustration to make sense, Job would had to have been able to understand the language and principles of construction. If God found this structure important enough to point out to Job, let's give some consideration to the construction of the pyramid and how it related to the earth, science, and mathematics in general.

THE WONDER OF THE PYRAMID

When fully intact the pyramid had more than two million stones, each weighing between 2.5 and 15 tons.[3] The mortar joints are consistently one-fiftieth of an inch.[4] The pyramid sits on a thirteen-acre flat mountain of solid granite.[5] That would cover an area of five city blocks. The pyramid rests in the exact center of the earth's landmass. The pyramid lies in the center of gravity of the continents. The pyramid is true north, offset by only three minutes of a degree. In contrast, the *Observatoire de Paris* constructed beginning in 1667 is off by six minutes.[6] This may not seem important until one considers that the building of these two edifices were separated by more than three and a half millennia and the Pyramid of Giza's offset can be relegated to a shift in the earth's polarity or to movement of the African tectonic plate.

The pyramid's measurements are astounding. The length of each side in Hebrew cubits is 365.2422—the equivalent to the number of days in a solar year. The pyramid's height is 232.52 cubits. When one takes twice the length of a side and divides it by the height, the result is 3.14159...also known as pi (π).[7]

The pyramid is visible from the moon. In its original state it was covered with tiles meant to reflect light and was said to have looked from space as a shining star. In fact, it was originally called *Ikhet*, which means "glorious light." The casing stones that covered it, 144,000 in all, were so brilliant that they could literally be seen from the mountains of Israel hundreds of miles away. On bright mornings and late afternoons, sunlight reflected by this vast mirrored surface of five and a quarter acres distinguished the pyramid as something one could have seen from the moon.[8]

All four sides of the pyramid are slightly bowed. The measurement of its curves is the exact curvature of the earth. The slope of the pyramid is ten to nine, meaning that for every ten feet in width, the walls rise in altitude nine feet. When we multiply the height of the pyramid in inches times ten to the ninth power, the result is 5,519,000,000 inches—or 91,840,270 miles, the number of miles for the mean distance from the sun to the earth.[9] Incidentally if we take the Hebrew characters of Isaiah 19:19–20, which many scholars believe makes reference to this pyramid, and add their numerical value, we get 5,449, which is the exact number of Hebrew inches of the height of the Great Pyramid! The volume of the pyramid could hold enough concrete to pave an eight-foot-wide path, four inches thick, from New York to San Francisco. In today's dollars, the raw material that makes up the pyramid alone would cost more than $100 million.

These are only a few of the wonders found in the pyramid's

measurements. It is obvious that the builder of the pyramid had to have had access to information far beyond the science of his time.

THE WORD AND THE PYRAMID

Two questions remain: first, is this Great Pyramid in the Bible? Though there is debate and some disagreement, scholars ancient and contemporary believe that the following passage is a reference to the Great Pyramid:

> In that day there will be an altar to the LORD in the midst of the land of Egypt, and a pillar to the LORD at its border. And it will be for a sign and for a witness to the LORD of hosts in the land of Egypt; for they will cry to the LORD because of the oppressors, and He will send them a Savior and a Mighty One, and He will deliver them. Then the LORD will be known to Egypt, and the Egyptians will know the LORD in that day, and will make sacrifice and offering; yes, they will make a vow to the LORD and perform it. And the LORD will strike Egypt, He will strike and heal it; they will return to the LORD, and He will be entreated by them and heal them.
>
> —ISAIAH 19:19–22

The purpose of the Great Pyramid is as a last days' witness to God's saving power. Note its location "in the midst of the land" and "at its border." The Great Pyramid sits in the exact center of Egypt. How can it be both on the border of the land and at the center? In those days (and even today) Egypt had a border between Lower and Upper Egypt. Lower Egypt is north, because the Nile River flows north into its delta. Upper Egypt is south. The pyramid sits exactly on the border. Even the word "Giza" means "border"!

Now the Bible says that this pillar and altar will reveal the Savior and the deliverance of Egypt! Also the Egyptian Arabs will hearken unto their ancestor Job and turn to their Redeemer!

David Davidson noted that the dynasty of Enoch was impressed upon the Great Pyramid itself.[10] Ancient writers called the Great Pyramid "the Pillar of Enoch." Enoch was in the line of Seth, who was the son of Adam and Eve, and the great historian Josephus ascribes the building of the Great Pyramid to the dynasty of Seth. We know that God revealed the plan of the tabernacle to Moses, so is it so far-fetched to believe that God would reveal a plan for this great testimony to someone like Enoch? In fact, is it so far-fetched to believe that God might have inspired and guided all the people concerned in the task? Consider what Jeremiah says about the Lord:

> Great in counsel, and mighty in work: for thine eyes are open upon all the ways of the sons of men: to give every one according to his ways, and according to the fruit of his doings: which has set signs and wonders in the land of Egypt, even unto this day.
>
> —JEREMIAH 32:19–20, KJV

THE WITNESS OF THE GREAT PYRAMID

This structure is astounding and certainly deserves our study. This is a wonder! This monument testifies to a Creator God! How? First, as has been previously mentioned, there is no way that the science of the day in which the pyramid was built could have given measurements so accurate in respect to the relationship between the pyramid's placement and the earth. That information had to come from an outside source.

Second, the pyramid bears witness to true science. As we have observed, this structure sets forth distances and measurements that could only have been known by an advanced civilization!

Third, the halls and chambers of the pyramid, when read in Hebrew inches, give a timeline that agrees with Bible history. The word *inch* comes from the name "Enoch," and Enoch was 365 years old when he was translated to heaven. The Jewish inch, the British inch, and the American inch are very similar, but they are not the same. When taking the Hebrew inch for a measurement, the chambers tell a remarkable story. We know that if we take the known dates inscribed on their walls, the pyramid measurement given accurately reflects the Exodus in 1453 BC and also points to AD 33—the Crucifixion. There are other remarkable dates, but time and space prohibit going into them here.

Finally, if you place a scale map on the pyramid over the map of Israel, the queen's chamber is at Bethlehem!

THE MYSTERY REVEALED

It bears mentioning that this pyramid has no capstone. Accounts from visitors as far back as the early first century after Christ agree in their report that the pyramid has always lacked a capstone. Some argue that it could have been looted, as capstones were often made of gold or silver, but the problem with this idea is that the capstone would have been too large to steal. One can freely walk around on the top of the pyramid, which is approximately thirty feet square.[11] Notice Job 38:6:

> To what were its foundations fastened? Or who laid its cornerstone?

And also Ephesians 2:21–22:

> In whom the whole building, being joined together, grows into a holy temple in the Lord, in whom you also are being built together for a dwelling place of God in the Spirit.

This capstone or "head cornerstone" is only found in a pyramid.[12] Consider Psalm 118:22:

> The stone which the builders rejected has become the chief cornerstone.

So much of the pyramid points to the supernatural—from its measurements and the science required to achieve knowledge of them to its external and internal construction and the way that it all points to and aligns with biblical history. We need only to look at the missing capstone to know that there is a final word to us from the Pyramid of Giza, and it is this: Jesus, the stone the builders rejected, is missing. But just as one who stands against all odds, He is weathered but still a wonder. And He will soon be back!

Chapter 4

The MYSTERY *of* SODOM *and* GOMORRAH

ODOM AND GOMORRAH. Their names induce immediate images of a people lost in such wickedness that the citizens of Rome at the height of their depravity might have blushed. The location of these cities, along with other "cities of the plain" (Gen. 19:29), has long been the subject of speculation and search. As most people who keep up with this type of thing know, there are several prevalent theories.

One is that the cities are today under the waters of the southern tip of the Dead Sea. Another is that they are located on the Jordanian shore of the Dead Sea on a plateau where five archeological sites have been located. However, these five sites are five hundred feet above the plain on a plateau, not *on* the plain, as is so specifically stated in the Bible. Also, they are far too small to have been cities—the largest is ten acres and the next largest is two acres.

THE FINDINGS

The Bible gives clues to the location of these cities:

> And the border of the Canaanites was from Sidon as you go toward Gerar, as far as Gaza; then as you go toward Sodom, Gomorrah, Admah, and Zeboiim, as far as Lasha.
>
> —GENESIS 10:19

With this information...

In the early 1980s Ron Wyatt noticed unusual formations on the shores of the Dead Sea. He said they looked like city walls but were white in color. These formations appeared in disparate locations more than fifty miles apart.

In 1989 Ron made a startling discovery. A road had been cut through some of these formations exposing the inner material that had collected in swirls, which suggested that these formations were not simply the result of geological layering. While visiting the site just below Masada, samples were taken of the material, which broke easily off of the main structures and disintegrated into something like the consistency of talcum powder. Ron's wife, Mary Nell, found a capsule, which turned out to be brimstone, embedded in a piece of compacted ash.

While exploring the site in October 1990, Ron Wyatt returned with Richard Rives and found areas of collapsed ash, wherein were found yellow balls surrounded by a reddish-black crust. These balls turned out to be encapsulated sulfur, or brimstone.[1]

Do these findings fit expectation?

The Bible tells the story of a conflagration in Genesis 19:24–25:

> Then the LORD rained brimstone and fire on Sodom and Gomorrah, from the LORD out of the heavens. So He overthrew those cities, all the plain, all the inhabitants of the cities, and what grew on the ground.

This inferno consumed the cities, with balls of brimstone raining down from the skies. This torrent of destruction completely annihilated the citizenry and turned the city's buildings to ash. We read in 2 Peter 2:6:

> And [God turned] the cities of Sodom and Gomorrah into ashes, condemned them to destruction, making them an example to those who afterward would live ungodly.

But this is not the only record of the remains of those cities. Josephus wrote:

> Now this country is then so sadly burnt up, that nobody cares to come at it.... It was of old a most happy land, both for the fruits it bore and the riches of its cities, although it be now all burnt up. It is related how, for the impiety of its inhabitants, it was burnt by lightning; in consequence of which *there are still the remainders of that divine fire; and the traces [or shadows] of the five cities are still to be seen.*[2]
>
> —EMPHASIS ADDED

This description by the noted and trustworthy historian Josephus describes perfectly what can be seen in the five ashen sites explored by Wyatt. These wan remains display all the visual characteristics of ancient cities and walls.

Noteworthy is the rapidity with which these cities would had to have been destroyed. When we compare two passages, we see first that the event did not begin until Lot and his family had not only left Sodom but were completely in Zoar:

> "Hurry, escape there. For I cannot do anything until you arrive there."
>
> Therefore the name of the city was called Zoar.
>
> *The sun had risen upon the earth* when Lot entered Zoar. Then the Lord rained brimstone and fire on Sodom and Gomorrah, from the Lord out of the heavens. So He overthrew those cities, all the plain, all the inhabitants of the cities, and what grew on the ground.
>
> —GENESIS 19:22–25, EMPHASIS ADDED

So the sun had already risen before the Lord began the obliteration of the cities. However, just a few verses later we read:

> And Abraham went *early in the morning* to the place where he had stood before the Lord. Then he looked toward Sodom

and Gomorrah, and toward all the land of the plain; and he saw, and behold, the smoke of the land which went up like the smoke of a furnace. And it came to pass, when God destroyed the cities of the plain, that God remembered Abraham, and sent Lot out of the midst of the overthrow, when He overthrew the cities in which Lot had dwelt.

—Genesis 19:27–29, emphasis added

As a shepherd Abraham would certainly have risen early to tend his flocks, but by the time Abraham rose from his slumber, the sky was already filled with the black smoke rising from the devastation of those cities. The event itself had already been completed.

Additionally it is important to notice that there is layering present in all of the ashen material at the sites. Thousands of layers are present, and none of these are very thick. In very high-temperature fires, or in very hot flames that contain alkali metals (e.g., sodium and calcium), the positive and negative ions attract and repel each other. This results in the demonstrated swirling layer effect. We know the flames must have been intensely hot in order to burn stone and metal, and there was and still is a high concentration of sodium in the region. The Dead Sea itself has the highest concentration of salt of any body of water on earth. The largest salt dome, Mount Sodom, is there in the region.

The area was covered with a kind of slime that was probably bitumen. This was a valuable commodity in those days. It was used as a preservative coating for burnt mud bricks as well as in mortar. In the Ebla tablets, found in Syria, there are listings of purchases, and the highest price paid, in silver, was for bitumen. All the people of these cities had to do was walk out their front door and collect the material. There was no need for them to work hard for it; it was plentiful.

THE SIN OF SODOM

Without question, the phrase "the sin of Sodom" is enough to cause lines to magically appear in the sand of any conversation. The easy answer is homosexuality. It is what we have been told in the church for decades, if not centuries. Even the word *sodomy* stems from this city's name. There is also scriptural basis for these claims. For example:

> And the LORD said, "Because the outcry against Sodom and Gomorrah is great, and because their sin is very grave..."
> —GENESIS 18:20

And later Abraham says to the Lord:

> "Far be it from You to do such a thing as this, to slay the righteous with the wicked, so that the righteous should be as the wicked; far be it from You! Shall not the Judge of all the earth do right?"
> So the LORD said, "If I find in Sodom fifty righteous within the city, then I will spare all the place for their sakes."
> —GENESIS 18:25–26

Their conversation goes as far as this:

> Then [Abraham] said, "Let not the LORD be angry, and I will speak but once more: Suppose ten should be found there?"
> And [the LORD] said, "I will not destroy it for the sake of ten."
> —GENESIS 18:32

The Lord could not even find ten righteous people in the city. So what was found there? We are told that angels of the Lord entered the city and went into Lot's house. And then:

> Now before they lay down, the men of the city, the men of Sodom, both old and young, all the people from every quarter, surrounded the house. And they called to Lot and said to him,

"Where are the men who came to you tonight? Bring them out to us that we may know them carnally."

—Genesis 19:4–5

And the final result was:

Then the Lord rained brimstone and fire on Sodom and Gomorrah, from the Lord out of the heavens. So He overthrew those cities, all the plain, all the inhabitants of the cities, and what grew on the ground.

—Genesis 19:24–25

So, there, plain as day, the sin of Sodom must have been homosexuality.

The problem, of course, is that we tend to latch onto homosexuality as the preeminent sin of Sodom because it is not ours. We can associate homosexuality with a sin worthy of destruction because "At least we don't sin like that." While it is true that homosexuality was rampant in the cities of the plain, and it is also true that homosexuality is a sin, the Bible actually provides some clarity for us on this issue.

You see, the real sin of Sodom is recorded in the Book of Ezekiel, where the prophet declares in an admonition against Jerusalem:

"As I live," says the Lord God, "neither your sister Sodom nor her daughters have done as you and your daughters have done. Look, this was the iniquity of your sister Sodom: She and her daughter had pride, fullness of food, and abundance of idleness; neither did she strengthen the hand of the poor and needy. And they were haughty and committed abomination before Me; therefore I took them away as I saw fit."

—Ezekiel 16:48–50

Look at those sins. Sodom was a city full of people who were prideful, wealthy, and idle, but in addition they had lost all concern for the poor and needy among them. They disregarded the hungry and homeless. This was a nation that was prosperous to the point of overflow, and their plenty had caused them to sink into the pointless pursuit of pleasure. They had cast off restraint, and they began to indulge in every conceivable vice and sin, to tolerate and even embrace those who committed any and all manner of perversion.

Does this sound like any country you know (or in which you may currently reside)?

THE SIGN OF SODOM

Why does this matter to us today? Well, aside from the obvious similarities to the United States and other formerly Christian countries around the world, Jesus Himself used Sodom as an illustration of the end times (much as He did with the days of Noah). He said:

> Likewise as it was also in the days of Lot: They ate, they drank, they bought, they sold, they planted, they built; but on the day that Lot went out of Sodom it rained fire and brimstone from heaven and destroyed them all. Even so will it be in the day when the Son of Man is revealed.
>
> In that day, he who is on the housetop, and his goods are in the house, let him not come down to take them away. And likewise the one who is in the field, let him not turn back. Remember Lot's wife.
>
> —LUKE 17:28–32

Jesus referred to Sodom's days as a shadow of the last days. But He was not alone in this, as Peter reminded the readers of his second epistle:

> And turning the cities of Sodom and Gomorrah into ashes, [God] condemned them to destruction, making them an example to those who afterward would live ungodly; and delivered righteous Lot, who was oppressed by the filthy conduct of the wicked.
>
> —2 PETER 2:6–7

Peter states that those cities were an example to those "who afterward would live ungodly." The word "example" here in the Greek is *hypodeigma*, which implies that it was something that could be seen by those then living. Jude continues with this idea, saying:

> Sodom and Gomorrah, and the cities around them in a similar manner to these, having given themselves over to sexual immorality and gone after strange flesh, are set forth as an example, suffering the vengeance of eternal fire.
>
> —JUDE 7

Jude also uses a word, in this case *deigma* (note the similar root to *hupodeigma*), that conveys the idea of being a visible thing.

THE MYSTERY REVEALED

Again we see that the discovery of these cities is an example of God bringing to bear the psalm and reminding us:

> Truth shall spring out of the earth, and righteousness shall look down from heaven.
>
> —PSALM 85:11

We court a dangerous foe when we allow sin to well up in our families, our communities, our nation, or ourselves. The danger of sin is that any sinful lifestyle inevitably starts with something innocuous. No one begins their descent into promiscuity by deciding to sleep with every person they encounter. No one becomes an alcoholic with their first sip of champagne. It is a gradual process.

This is what happened in Sodom and Gomorrah. At some point in history these cities were nothing more than a gathering of people. Then they found the mineral wealth all around them. After that came growth, then affluence, then the lethargy of prosperity. At some point, out of all that, the people of these cities came to a sense of entitlement. They stopped caring for the poor. They began to think only of themselves and their own pleasure. It was this mind-set that caused them to look at two strangers in town not as travelers to whom basic hospitality was owed but as two bodies that the citizens of Sodom had a right to use as they saw fit.

Sodom still speaks to us today. No longer can we simply turn a blind eye and a deaf ear to the sin around us, whether that sin is homosexuality, gossip, adultery, fornication, murder (in reality or in speech and thought), pride, callous disregard of those less fortunate than us, refusal to care for the hungry and the needy, or what have you. Sin must be addressed. Sodom, Gomorrah, and the cities of the plain stand as a testament to us today that there is a natural outgrowth of what we might deem lesser sins and that there is a judgment to be faced for our folly.

Chapter 5

The MYSTERY *of* MELCHIZEDEK

IN THE ANCIENT account of Job we find a poignant passage in which the deep longings of Job's heart are expressed:

> For He is not a man, as I am, that I may answer Him, and that we should go to court together. Nor is there any mediator between us, who may lay his hand on us both. Let Him take His rod away from me, and do not let dread of Him terrify me. Then I would speak and not fear Him, but it is not so with me.
> —JOB 9:32–35

Job's desire is for an audience with the Almighty, but Job knows he is unworthy. He longs, then, for a mediator; a great High Priest who would be worthy to touch both God and man; a Savior who was, indeed, fully God and fully man. What Job cried for was fulfilled in Jesus Christ. He is our great High Priest and stands beside us to ensure our connection to the Father.

The Book of Hebrews declares this glorious truth. In Hebrews 2:17 Jesus is called our "merciful and faithful High Priest." In Hebrews 4:15–16 we read that Christ was "in all points tempted as we are, yet without sin...that we may obtain mercy and find grace to help in time of need."

Jesus was a priest according to the order of Melchizedek. This is problematic to the Jewish way of thinking, which would say, "We already have a priesthood—the Aaronic and Levitical priesthood. Jesus was not in the existing priestly line. How can He be our

32

priest?" What is it about the order of Melchizedek that is so special that Jesus was ordained in that manner?

Shrouded in Mystery

Melchizedek appears quite suddenly in the pages of Genesis after Abraham's defeat of Kedorlaomer, the great king of Elam. Melchizedek arrives, and Abraham, almost inexplicably, chooses to honor this king-priest from the city of Salem, which according to Josephus is the ancient name of Jerusalem.

Hebrews 7:3 points out that Melchizedek was not a priest by descent but by divine call:

> Without father, without mother, without genealogy, having neither beginning of days nor end of life, but made like the Son of God, [he] remains a priest continually.

This phrase "without father, without mother" does not mean that he sprang miraculously from the ground. It simply is a way of prefacing the phrase "without genealogy" so as to indicate that Melchizedek was not a priest or king due to his lineage but that he received a special ordination to be "made like the Son of God." Jesus was not a reflection of Melchizedek, but rather Melchizedek was like Jesus, a foreshadowing. God called Melchizedek out and gave him a ministry that was filled with hope, much as Jesus would proclaim in His mission years later. No wonder Jesus said, "Your father Abraham rejoiced to see My day" (John 8:56). When Abraham saw Melchizedek, he, Abraham, saw one like Jesus.

In the ancient Book of Jasher, cited as history twice in the Old Testament, it is declared that Shem, Noah's son, was Melchizedek. Also, it says that Abraham lived with Noah's family for a season as a refugee from the evil designs of the Babylonians. It is amazing to consider that Noah talked with Adam and that Shem, obviously, talked with Noah. Abraham, then, even though removed from the event by eleven generations, would have experienced a firsthand account of God's salvation in Noah's family.[1]

The Order Is Stronger in Ministry

Aside from the account in Genesis Melchizedek is mentioned in only one other place in the Old Testament: Psalm 110, a psalm of David that proclaims the announcement of the reign of the Messiah. This psalm is quoted in Hebrews 5:6, 5:10, 6:20, 7:17, and 7:21. This psalm declares that the coming Messiah will be "a priest for ever after the order of Melchizedek" (Ps. 110:4, KJV).

In the Genesis 14 account Abraham had just returned from a great victory over four kings. He had rescued his nephew Lot and helped the king of Sodom, and the grateful king wished to offer riches to Abraham. God knew that Abraham would need strength to face that temptation, so God sent the king of Salem, Melchizedek, to Abraham's camp. In Genesis 14:18 Melchizedek brought bread and wine. These are the symbols of the price of victory. Both body and blood were sacrificed when a victory was obtained. Melchizedek came to remind Abraham that it was the Most High God, El Elyon, who had given him the victory. Melchizedek then blessed Abraham, and Abraham gave a tithe to God as recognition of God's ownership of everything in his life.

You see, the king of Sodom had intended to offer Abraham worldly riches. God sent Melchizedek to remind Abraham that true wealth and victory consist not in the riches of this world but in God's blessing. Because Abraham refused to take credit for the victory and turned down the reward of the world, God appeared to him and said, "Do not be afraid, Abram. I am your shield, your exceedingly great reward" (Gen. 15:1).

The Mystery Revealed

Abraham tithed long before God set forth the laws of giving and tithing. From this story we also learn that the giving of our tithe is an acknowledgement of Jesus's victory and ownership of all. But more importantly this ancient mystery beautifully pictures the ministry of our Lord Jesus. He is our King of righteousness, but He is also, when we receive Him, our King of peace. Christ is the source of our victory. Every time we partake of the bread and wine of Holy Communion, we remember Jesus's victory on Calvary, and that victory is what enables us to walk in victory today. It is to Jesus, and not the world, to whom we owe our loyalty.

Chapter 6

The MYSTERY *of* LOST ATLANTIS

THE WORLD IN which we live is replete with mysteries. For years science has promoted uniformitarianism. This is the "assumption that the same natural laws and processes that operate in the universe now have always operated in the universe in the past and apply everywhere in the universe."[1] Essentially this idea teaches that earth's history has progressed across the centuries in a uniform and predictable way.

However, scientists in various fields and of various worldviews are, with greater frequency, embracing the idea of catastrophism. More and more scientists are accepting the truth that the earth has been subjected to various catastrophes throughout its history. This both explains and deepens the mystery of earth's history.

The Bible is the first source of teaching that dramatic catastrophes have marked the history of the earth. Look at just a few that are mentioned in Scripture:

- The original global catastrophe in Genesis 1:1–2

- The global deluge of Noah's flood

- The destruction of the cities of the plain

- The miracles, disasters, and plagues accompanying the Exodus

Throughout Scripture there are references to volcanoes, earthquakes, and other disasters. The earth itself is dotted with ruins that have no historical reference or explanation. The great civilizations of South America, Stonehenge, Easter Island, and others are called megalithic ruins, and they dot the landscape of our planet.

From these and others, mysteries and stories have come down to us. Today we often refer to them as myths. Yet in all of them we find a kernel of truth.

THE LOST CITY

For over a year I had studied the fabled Atlantis, not knowing that I had actually been there. Located in the azure waters of the Aegean Sea is a place so lovely that it nearly defies description. Kathleen Burke, in an article written for *Smithsonian* magazine, has called it a "must see" location and quoted this description of it by Lawrence Durrell:

> It is hardly a matter of surprise that few, if any, good descriptions of Santorini have been written: the reality is so astonishing that prose and poetry, however winged, will forever be forced to limp behind.[2]

I have visited the island now known as Santorini, whose ancient name is Thera, and I can concur with her words.

This island was once a part of a thriving Minoan culture that traded with all of the known world. It was very wealthy and influential. Frescoes from the excavations of Akrotiri, a city on the island, show that it was a place of exotic spices, fishing trade, athletics, and art. This city, like Pompeii so many years later, was devoured by a volcanic explosion so quickly that it is nearly perfectly preserved under sixteen feet of volcanic ash.

In his work *Timaeus* Plato wrote of the story of Solon's journey to Egypt. It was here that he, Solon, first heard the story of Atlantis from an Egyptian priest. The interesting thing to note is that if we move Plato's dates for these events by one decimal point and then divide the measurements and age of Atlantis by ten, we come up with the dimensions of the island of Santorini before the great volcanic explosion of 1450 BC.[3]

Atlantis was reported to be a circular island with an inland circle of water and a populated plain. If we consider what geologists tell us about Santorini, the description fits perfectly.

The Bible and Atlantis

I know what you're thinking. Right now it's one of two things: "How interesting, but so what?" or "So what?" Why is this of any interest to believers? What we have to note is that the dating of this catastrophe is of enormous significance to believers. You see, the proper dating of this Atlantean destruction places it during the end of the captivity of Israel in Egypt and just prior to the Exodus. That God used this event as part of the judgment of Egypt is more than likely.

So What Happened?

The island of Santorini is located between the continental plates of Europe and Africa. There was, at first, a massive earthquake that opened up the earth, allowing seawater to pour into the thirteen-hundred-foot caldera (the hot center of the volcano that originated the island). This water rushing in caused the volcano to steam, to enlarge, and, finally, to explode. The estimates are that Thera's explosion was sixteen hundred times more powerful than the hydrogen bomb created at Eniwetok.[4] One hundred fifty-three square miles of city, plains, and earth were vaporized in an instant!

The subsequent results are staggering. In thirty minutes a tsunami between two and three hundred feet high hit the island of Crete at approximately three hundred miles per hour! In a matter of hours, waves as high as eighty feet could have hit the shores of Northern Africa. Thick ash covered much of the Mediterranean area. The darkness that fell on Egypt during the time of the plagues was likely caused by ash.[5]

As the explosion was thousands of times stronger than the

eruption of Mount St. Helens in AD 1980, we know that this disaster affected the whole world. When the Krakatoa volcano erupted in 1883, the sound was heard in Australia and registered in Potsdom, Germany. The resultant tidal waves killed thirty-six thousand in Java and Sumatra. Those same waves circled the earth twice. To put it in perspective, the Theran eruption was five times stronger than the eruption at Krakatoa.[6]

Tree-ring data shows that the Thera eruption probably caused a growth depression of European oaks in Ireland and Scotch pines in Sweden. Bristlecone pine frost rings show the event and the effects on trees were felt as far away as North America. *The Bamboo Annals*, a chronicle of ancient China, relates how in 1618 BC there was a kind of volcanic winter accompanied by "yellow fog, a dim sun, then three suns, frost in July, famine, and the withering of all five cereals."[7]

THE MYSTERY REVEALED

If all of this is known, then what is the mystery? Well, there are theories that the great empire of Egypt had, as its origin, the people of Santorini, and that this eruption, which affected so much of the known world and had very real impact on the plagues of Egypt, was, in fact, a judgment upon Egypt at its origin.

More than any of that, however, there is this: God still speaks out of a mystery!

There is, simply, a lot we do not know. I have said already that I make no claim that my understanding of these mysteries is the inerrant truth. Where I state my opinion, I try to make that clear, but I also show that there are other understandings and theories. But there is a movement among some so-called scientists that would have you and me believe that their latest discovery is rock-solid truth. Dear friend, history has shown us over and over again that this is simply not so. Why? Because...

God is sovereign over His planet. We have to understand that the Creator is in control of the creation. It is simple as that. Also, we look to Atlantis (as well as Sodom and Gomorrah, the Egypt of Exodus, Jericho, and the other wicked empires of Canaan) and are reminded that God's judgments are sweeping and powerful. We forget this at our peril, because, as we read again and again in the Bible, man is dependent on God.

The good news of this story is that God is willing to use extreme measures to rescue those who are His. If it means turning a nation's water supply to blood, infesting the land with locusts, or causing an eruption that levels an island, God will never forsake those who are His. But to be His, a person needs to be right with God. We know from history that we cannot do it on our own, so God made a way for us Himself.

Finally, we learn that all human endeavor is temporary. All that we do, all that we hope to achieve or attain can be wiped away in a moment, and it is only those things that glorify God that will remain.

Chapter 7

The MYSTERY *of the* ANGELS

THERE ARE MANY misconceptions about miracles. While this is not the place for an exhaustive explanation of miracles, their existence, their purpose, or their power, it is important that there be an acknowledgement that miracles *are*. Miracles still happen today, and as important as it is that we acknowledge their existence, we need also to understand how they occur. Simply put, a miracle is a dimensional interruption whereby God breaks into our mundane existence and changes our lives from ordinary to extraordinary. It is a thing of wonder, and we can, and should, live in wonder again!*

People have asked me why I still believe that God performs miracles. For me the answer is a simple one.

It was my very first year of college at Clarke College in Newton, Mississippi. I was driving my 1956 Chevrolet back to Newton on old Highway 80 out of Selma, Alabama, toward Uniontown. This road is now an expansive four-lane highway, but back then it was a tiny two-lane thoroughfare that was lucky to have pavement. Suddenly there was a car coming at me in my lane. To this day I am not certain why he appeared there. All I know for certain is that we were headed toward an inescapable head-on collision. When I looked to the right, I saw nothing but an impenetrable concrete bridge abutment. In the fast thinking that happens only in those life-or-death moments, I decided that trying to scrape by the abutment was a

---

* Portions of this chapter have been adapted from *Our Invisible Allies* by Ron Phillips.

better choice than a head-on collision. I closed my eyes and veered to the right in an effort to take my chances with the concrete bulwark. Suddenly I was on the other side. I missed the oncoming car on the bridge, and I went on my way! I know I was not speeding, and I know that God protected me.

Some will call me crazy, but I have always thought that an angel lifted my car and set it down. There is no reason in this world that my car or I should have come out of that moment unscathed, but we did. I know I live in a world where miraculous things happen. As I sat in that car, shaking from the rush of adrenaline coursing through my body, my thoughts turned with lighting speed from thanksgiving to hilarity to wonder and back again. I remember thinking almost simultaneously, "Thank You, God!" and "Why would You bother saving me, God?" It makes me remember the great psalm:

> When I consider Your heavens, the work of Your fingers, the moon and the stars, which You have ordained, what is man that You are mindful of him, and the son of man that You visit him?
>
> —Psalm 8:3–4

I imagine David, the shepherd, sitting under the stars in the Judean wilderness after an exhausting day of herding sheep, when suddenly the splendor of the sky overwhelms him. In that moment he sees the utter insignificance of man put into sharp contrast with the vast mystery of God. David's heart explodes in wonder and praise that God would take time to give thought to man. Beyond that David sees a God who is coming for man.

This is the height of human glory! Our God takes notice of us, cares for us, and crowns us as royalty on earth. However, in this psalm David reveals to us that our universe, as vast as it is, is not the only realm where life abounds. Life exists in other dimensions beyond the earth! In fact, supernatural beings exist beyond our earthly realm. Speaking of humanity, the Bible says, "For You have made him a little lower than the angels" (Ps. 8:5). David looked heavenward and saw the majesty of God in the vastness of the created order! He looked to earth and saw tiny man as the centerpiece and crowning glory of that order. We can hear the music of the eternal and its rhythm soaring from his ravished soul.

THE REVELATION OF ANGELS

There are other beings from another dimension that are moving by the multitudes across the vast expanse of our known world. These beings are not subject to the limitations of our world. Beyond our normal range of understanding is another dimension more real and lasting than anything we can imagine. The existence of another realm called "the heavenlies," where marvelous creatures, both magnificent and malevolent, operate, is not science fiction. In this realm these living beings called angels, along with their dark cousins demons, exist. Both were created by God, and these timeless beings have a history of their own.

There is no one section of the Bible that tells us all about angels. We have to cull the various references and make sense of them as best we can. To start, let's examine a passage in Nehemiah:

> You alone are the LORD; You have made heaven, the heaven of heavens, with all their host, the earth and everything on it, the seas and all that is in them, and You preserve them all. The host of heaven worships You.
> —NEHEMIAH 9:6

There is a lot to unpack here. Nehemiah establishes the fundamental truth that God is the only God. The prophet then says that God made heaven *and* "the heaven of heavens." What is this place, and why does Nehemiah make the distinction?

There are three realms in the Bible that are referred to as "heaven." There is, first, our atmosphere. That is easy enough to understand. Second, the area above our atmosphere, where there are moons and stars and other planets, is referred to as "heaven." But there is a "heaven of heavens." This place, called *shamayi h'shamayim*, is mentioned in Genesis 28, Deuteronomy 10, 1 Kings 8, and other passages as a distinct and completely spiritual realm. It is also mentioned in 2 Corinthians 12:2–4, where the apostle Paul wrote:

> I know a man in Christ who fourteen years ago—whether in the body I do not know, or whether out of the body I do not know, God knows—such a one was caught up to the third heaven. And I know such a man—whether in the body or out of the body I do not know, God knows—how he was caught up into Paradise and heard inexpressible words, which it is not lawful for a man to utter.

The Greek says that the man was "caught away," not "caught up." This reflects the Jewish belief that Paradise was somewhere other than the uppermost heaven.

Yahweh, the Lord, created all the "hosts of heaven," and these "hosts" worship Him. Angels came to life at the command of God. Psalm 148:5 says that they are to "praise the name of the LORD, for He commanded and they were created." These wonderful creatures are of a number so vast, I dare say they could not be counted. Our universe, in the vastness of its expanse, seems empty of life, but the heavenly realm teems with energy and life.

Psalm 148 indicates that the angels were in existence prior to the creation of the sun, moon, and stars. Their function was to praise and worship the Lord. Paul affirms this in his letter to the Colossians when he says:

> For by Him [Jesus] all things were created that are in heaven and that are on earth, visible and invisible, whether thrones or dominions or principalities or powers. All things were created through Him and for Him.
>
> —Colossians 1:16

Angels were created by the Lord Jesus and for the Lord Jesus. Further, they were present at the creation of our realm. In the Book of Job the Lord chastises Job and asks him:

> Where were you when I laid the foundations of the earth? Tell Me, if you have understanding. Who determined its measurements? Surely you know! Or who stretched the line upon it? To what were its foundations fastened? Or who laid its cornerstone, when the morning stars sang together, and all the sons of God shouted for joy?
>
> —JOB 38:4-7

Job may very well be the oldest book of the Bible. It is full of wonder and mystery. According to the Scripture passage here, angels were active at the dawn of creation. When I read these words, my soul trembles within me; we read and are carried back to the earliest moments of history.

Creation, in what scientists call the Big Bang, was initiated by the mighty sound of God's voice breaking through every dimension. As the great starry host exploded in a fireworks display, the remnant of that explosion still lights up the sky over our heads. Our sun still warms us all these ages later from that beginning blast. Watching this demonstration, like a family at a fireworks display, were the "sons of God," the angels. All of these beings shouted and sang while the creation was being strung into place by God's hand. The stars were their orchestra as they shouted with joy!

Earth is a small planet in an average-sized solar system on the edge of a galaxy called the Milky Way. The vast expanse of the universe dwarfs our planet. In the comparison the earth would be smaller than a grain of sand in a large building. That perspective diminishes the significance of those of us who live on Sagan's "pale blue dot."

But you see, if the visible world is all there is and life is an accident, then human intelligence, achievements, and aspirations mean nothing. Solomon felt this after exploring human existence in the present dimension and declared it to be "grasping for the wind" (Eccles. 1:17). Solomon understood that God has set a desire in humanity for more than what we can see in this life. His quest left him to discover the eternal dimension, a reality beyond the four dimensions of our existence. From Ecclesiastes 3:11 we see this perspective in the eternal Word:

> [God] has made everything beautiful in its time. Also He has
> put eternity in their hearts, except that no one can find out
> the work that God does from beginning to end.

Solomon understood that God has made everything beautiful in its time. It is God who put eternity in our hearts, and the work that God does from beginning to end is on His time schedule. We should rejoice and do well in our lives, and eat and drink and enjoy the good of our labor here on earth, because it is the gift of God. Our lives are connected to an eternal world more real and lasting than this present world.

There are some who would disagree with me, but I believe *The Matrix* film demonstrates this truth better than any attempt I could make. This movie was fascinating, as the characters were living in an artificial world that they thought was real. The first film chronicles the discovery that he is asleep to the real world, is being manipulated by evil forces, and is a prisoner of this dark world. In his attempt to discover the unseen real world, he is ridiculed and mocked. He has to experience a kind of death to reveal the true world.

This scenario is true of our world. It is temporary! We live in a dimension that, while real, is not eternal! We can escape this realm and live in the heavenly dimension where angels operate and miracles happen. Paul made this discovery two thousand years ago and declared it to the church in Corinth:

> Therefore we do not lose heart. Even though our outward man
> is perishing, yet the inward man is being renewed day by day.
> For our light affliction, which is but for a moment, is working

for us a far more exceeding and eternal weight of glory, while we do not look at the things which are seen, but at the things which are not seen. For the things which are seen are temporary, but the things which are not seen are eternal.

—2 CORINTHIANS 4:16–18

There is an unseen world that is greater, more real, and more lasting than our limited existence.

THE RANKS

So how does God operate in our world? He moves through people and angels! I have already mentioned Nehemiah 9:6. Recall that in that passage Nehemiah refers to *hosts*. This name has to do with the vast number of these spiritual beings available to serve. How many angels are there exactly? No one except God could count them. Take note of some verses that reference their number:

The chariots of God are twenty thousand, even thousands of thousands.

—PSALM 68:17

…an innumerable company of angels.

—HEBREWS 12:22

And the number of them was ten thousand times ten thousand, and thousands of thousands.

—REVELATION 5:11

The point here is that there are plenty of those wonderful friends available to help us at just the right moment.

Angels

Angels are our supernatural allies. They have incredibly high intelligence, and they are part of our kingdom family. In Hebrews 12:22 we read that the "innumerable company of angels" gathered was there to join with the church in worship. But is that all the angels do?

In the New Testament the English word *angel* comes from the Greek word *aggelos*, which means "a messenger" or "one who heralds." In the Old Testament the word translated *"angel"* is *malak*, which means "a message sent." This, of course, indicates that God uses angels to communicate.

All of us are aware of the financial meltdown in late 2008. Two weeks before the crisis really broke, I was praying in my basement study, when I felt a breeze and a presence in the room. As I prayed, I heard in my spirit a voice saying, "Make your retirement safe!" Instead of obeying, I called my representative at our Christian retirement agency, and he advised against moving the money. Consequently, I experienced a loss, as did most of the country. I am firmly convinced that God sent an angel to advise me, and I did not listen.

Sons of God

Angels are also called "sons of God" in various places in Scripture. This title is primarily used in the Old Testament, and it speaks primarily of the angels' relationship with God the Father. Recall in Job 2:1 where we are told that there was a "day when the sons of God came to present themselves before the LORD."

Now before I go further in this chapter, it is important that I be very clear. We are not to worship angels! Anyone who tells you differently is preaching blasphemy. Angels are "unbegotten" sons of God, while Jesus is the "only begotten" Son of God (John 3:16). Angels are sons of God in the same way that we are when John wrote, "Beloved, now we are the sons of God" (1 John 3:2, KJV). God is father to us all, and if you have accepted Christ as your Savior, then you are part of an eternal cosmic family.

Cherubim

Every angel has a specific task, and there is a class of angels called cherubim whose job it is to guard the throne of God upon the earth. It appears from what we read in Scripture that the cherubim accompany God when He manifests Himself on earth.

Cherubim are first mentioned, however, in Genesis 3:24 when they are placed east of Eden to guard the way to the tree of life. This is very interesting, because the word *cherubim* comes from an ancient word that means "great, mighty, and gracious to bless."[1] These are clearly the attributes of God! There at Eden it would seem that these cherubim are hostile to humans in that they guard the way, or block access to, the tree of life. On the contrary, they are exhibiting grace, for if Adam were to eat from that tree, he would have been cursed to live in an aging body forever. It was grace that set the cherubim there for us.

I believe Adam and his family brought their offering to the gates of Eden where these cherubim were stationed. Here a bloody sacrifice was offered by our ancient family. It is interesting to see later in Scripture that cherubim of gold adorned the holy of holies around the mercy seat in the tabernacle and temple. They also adorned the ark of the covenant. These beautiful creatures were a reminder of all that was lost beyond the garden gate and of man's need for a Savior.

The real cherubim abode in the tabernacle when the cloud of glory, called the Shekinah, appeared above the mercy seat. Angels guarded the presence of God. When God was not honored, angels were activated to defend God's throne.

Recall God's word to Moses:

> And there I will meet with you, and I will speak with you from above the mercy seat, from between the two cherubim which are on the ark of the Testimony, about everything which I will give you in commandment to the children of Israel.
>
> —EXODUS 25:22

These cherubim later appear in the Book of Ezekiel in chapter 10. Each of them is described as having wings, wheels as a means of conveyance, and four faces. This would seem to go along with the idea of God's chariot drivers transporting God's throne on earth! Later these same beings are observed in Revelation 4 and are called "living ones" in English, and in Greek *zoon*. From this word we get our English word *zoo*. Cherubim, then, are angelic forces related to Planet Earth and its creative order. The four faces exhibit this truth, as the number four traditionally represents the earth.

Seraphim

Some of the heavenly beings are called seraphim. This name is only found in Isaiah 6, when the great prophet had his transforming vision. Isaiah's king and cousin Uzziah had died, and the prophet went into the forbidden holy of holies. In his grief he needed a word from God, even if it cost him his life. Upon entering the holy of holies, Isaiah saw the Lord high and lifted up in majesty and glory! In this place seraphim worshipped God, crying, "Holy, holy, holy!" As Isaiah looked upon this scene, he was provoked to declare his own unworthiness. A seraph brought a coal of fire from the altar, where the blood sacrifice burned, and placed it upon the prophet's lips. The fire cleansed him and redirected his life!

Seraphim, you see, means, "burning ones." It would appear that there is a direct link between these angels and the manifest presence of God. These are the beings that set our hearts on fire for God's holiness, His presence, and His power. (See Isaiah 6:1–7.)

Michael

Michael, whose name means "Who is like God?" is mentioned in both the Old and New Testaments. We discover in these passages that he is the commander and chief of the angelic armies of earth. In the Book of Daniel, it is Michael who wars against the demonic prince of Persia for two weeks in order to answer Daniel's prayers. (See Daniel 10:13.) Michael is also found in Revelation 12:7

at the end of the age as the one who casts Satan and the fallen angels out of the heavenlies. In today's vernacular Michael would be known as the secretary of war.

Gabriel

This mighty angel shows up to answer prayer, interpret dreams, and release the word of God. If Michael is secretary of war, then Gabriel is vice president of communications. Gabriel interpreted dreams for Daniel on two separate occasions. He also brought the word to Mary that even though she was a virgin, she would bear a child, Jesus the Son of God. Gabriel said of himself that he "stands in the presence of God" (Luke 1:19). This indicates that, along with Michael, Gabriel is the highest rank of angelic authority.

Could this angel have a special assignment to watch over salvation? In Isaiah 63:9 we read, "In all their affliction He was afflicted, and the Angel of His Presence saved them." Some believe the angel of His presence is the pre-incarnate Christ, but clearly this angel is Gabriel.

Angel of the Lord

The term "angel of the Lord" is mentioned sixty-three times in Scripture. Like the angel of His presence, many believe that this angel is the pre-incarnate Christ. This is impossible, as the angel appears twelve times in the New Testament. This angel and the angel of His presence could possibly be the same being. This angel carries an awesome anointing, so much so that God's presence is recognized, then worshipped, whenever this angel appears. This leads me to believe that this angel is God's accompanying angel.

Additionally the angel of the Lord has mighty power. He knows and operates on behalf of the people who dwell in the presence of God. It was this angel who stayed the hand of Abraham from killing Isaac; who stretched his sword over Jerusalem, causing its destruction in David's day; who killed the 185,000 of the Assyrian army in one night; who ordered the watching angels to do surveillance of the whole earth in the Book of Zechariah. Also we see that the angel of the Lord directed the heavenly choir over the shepherds' field in Bethlehem, appeared to Joseph and Mary to guide them to safety in Egypt, and struck Peter to awaken him and lead him out of prison.

Principalities, powers, thrones, and dominions

These are titles of angels who rank over regions, nations, cities, and communities. These can be either good or evil beings. There is a struggle in the invisible realm, known as the heavenlies, between angels of light and those of darkness. This struggle is affected by our prayers. (See Daniel 10; Ephesians 6:12; James 5:16.)

All angels have names, distinct personalities, and specific assignments. As the church comes to the end of herself and realizes the impossibility of her task against the threat of demonic terror and the rising opposition of a secular society, she will engage the supernatural resources available from God. The church will discover an open heaven, and the hosts, the angelic armies, will come to her aid.

Angelic Realms

There are realms of reality and life beyond human reach and reason. The angels, God's hosts, are among such mysteries. Yet these supernatural beings are found throughout the Scriptures, from the first page to the last page of the Bible.

Throughout my life I have been the recipient of angelic assistance. Only recently has science begun to catch up with the Bible in the area of other realms and dimensions beyond normal human perception. Living with us and beyond us at the same time are angels of God.

The unseen world

Quantum physics studies the origin of matter. This realm of science believes the world had a beginning; therefore a greater world existed and still thrives beyond our cosmos. On earth we live in four dimensions: we live in a world with length, width, height, and time. In the natural these dimensions limit us. Quantum physicists such as Brian Greene, who wrote *The Elegant Universe*, have discovered the existence of at least eleven dimensions. All of these dimensions are moving in straight lines. This perspective, or history, is called "linear." God created our universe and set this line in motion. He created it, but He is not captive to it. God lives above and beyond our history. Knowing that there are at least seven other dimensions beyond our limited view, our perspective is broadened, and dimensions we have not seen captivate our imagination.

This is the realm where God abides! Paul called these dimensions "the third heaven." Solomon, at the dedication of the great temple, spoke of our God not being limited to the heavens we observe. He said, "But will God indeed dwell on the earth? Behold, heaven and the heaven of heavens cannot contain You. How much less this temple which I have built!" (1 Kings 8:27).

How do we reach the dimension where God dwells? Our linear history cannot reach the third heaven. Our dimensions simply do not travel in the same direction. However, His dimension may intersect with ours. When that happens, all that is in the new (or God) dimension, according to quantum physics, becomes available in our present dimension. When these dimensions intersect, the limitations and laws of our present dimension can be altered, broken, or transformed. The limits and laws of our four-dimensional world can be suspended. Our natural order can be changed by a supernatural dimensional interruption.

THE MYSTERY REVEALED

Billy Graham once said:

> Angels belong to a uniquely different dimension of creation that we, limited to the natural order, can scarcely comprehend. In this angelic domain the limitations are different

from those God has imposed on our natural order. He has given angels higher knowledge, power, and mobility than we; they are God's messengers whose chief business is to carry out His orders in the world. He has given them an ambassadorial charge. He has designated and empowered them as holy deputies to perform works of righteousness. In this way they assist Him as their Creator, while His sovereignty controls the universe. So He has given them the capacity to bring His holy enterprises to a successful conclusion.[2]

Long before *Star Wars* the ancient prophets saw an end-time life-and-death struggle between the forces of darkness and the forces of light in the eternal realm. Though the war has been won by Christ at the cross, a battle rages for the soul of mankind; we are not alone in that battle. We have invisible allies available to assist us in the end time as we enforce Christ's victory.

Chapter 8

The MYSTERY *of* MOUNT SINAI

OUNT SINAI: THAT enigmatic rock in the desert where God met with His children. Cecil B. DeMille captured its majesty in his epic *The Ten Commandments* and in so doing solidified the picture of its grandeur for a generation of Christians. But what do we know about this geographical landmark? Moreover does this mountain have any relevance to Christians today? Apparently the apostle Paul thought so. Read his words to the Corinthians found in 1 Corinthians 10:1–10:

> Moreover, brethren, I do not want you to be unaware that all our fathers were under the cloud, all passed through the sea, all were baptized into Moses in the cloud and in the sea, all ate the same spiritual food, and all drank the same spiritual drink. For they drank of that spiritual Rock that followed them, and that Rock was Christ. But with most of them God was not well pleased, for their bodies were scattered in the wilderness.
>
> Now these things became our examples, to the intent that we should not lust after evil things as they also lusted. And do not become idolaters as were some of them. As it is written, "The people sat down to eat and drink, and rose up to play." Nor let us commit sexual immorality, as some of them did, and in one day twenty-three thousand fell; nor let us tempt Christ, as some of them also tempted, and were destroyed by serpents; nor complain, as some of them also complained, and were destroyed by the destroyer.

Paul remembered these events of the Exodus and marked them, not only for the Corinthians, but also for you and me today. Why would he do this? There are many reasons, but for our purposes here it is important to note verse 6 as well as verse 11 (which follows the passage above). Paul says:

> Now all these things happened to them as examples, and they were written for our admonition, upon whom the ends of the ages have come.
> —1 Corinthians 10:11

Like Sodom and Gomorrah, like Noah's ark, like the ark of the covenant, which will be discussed in a later chapter, Mount Sinai itself and the events that happened there are examples to us, reminders to us of the truth of God's Word, warnings that reflect the imminent Second Coming.

The Route of the Exodus

One of the astounding discoveries of our day is the real route of the Exodus and the location of Mount Sinai. For years people have believed that God's mountain is in the Sinai Peninsula. It makes sense, I suppose, what with it being called the "Sinai" Peninsula, but there is one major problem with this location: it is still in Egypt! God had clearly called His people out of Egypt, so to bring them to a place that was still Egypt, which was easily accessible from the Nile Delta, which would have been garrisoned with Egyptian armies, is not only contrary to what He called them to do, but also it is ridiculously illogical.

Midian

To better understand where Sinai is, we have to go back to years before the Exodus happened. Back to when Moses was just a fugitive murderer trying to turn his life around. He had married into a fairly wealthy house. His father-in-law, Jethro, was a priest in the land of Midian. Moses had rescued Jethro's daughters from some hooligan shepherds and been rewarded with a wife, Zipporah. Moses then became a shepherd for his father-in-law, and it was while tending sheep, in *Midian*, that Moses, at the base of Mount Horeb, saw a bush that burned but was not consumed. Here, we are told in Exodus 3:12, God said to Moses:

> I will certainly be with you. And this shall be a sign to you that I have sent you: When you have brought the people out of Egypt, you shall serve God *on this mountain*.
>
> —EMPHASIS ADDED

Here we have the first and best clue about the location of Sinai. It is in the land of Jethro, the land of Moses's father-in-law, which we are told clearly is the land of Midian. Moses was told to bring them back to this mountain where God had spoken to him. This mountain is not in the Sinai Peninsula but in northwestern Saudi Arabia.

But this is just me talking, right? I'm no archaeologist. Is there anything, especially in the Bible, that would back up this wild claim I have that Mount Sinai is not on the peninsula that bears its name but is, instead, on the mainland of the Arabian Peninsula? Why, yes, there is! In his letter to the Galatians, Paul said:

> For this Agar is mount Sinai in Arabia, and answereth to Jerusalem which now is, and is in bondage with her children.
>
> —GALATIANS 4:25, KJV

Throughout the Sinai Peninsula there is a tremendous amount of evidence of the ancient Egyptians having control of this area. Inscriptions tell of their mining operations there. There are temples as well as fortresses there. I say again, if Moses had led the people to the Sinai Peninsula and stopped, they would still have been in Egypt! However, there is no evidence of Egyptian occupation in Saudi Arabia.

Rameses

Unlike the commonly held thought, Rameses was not a city. It was the Delta region, the land given to Joseph's family to live in by the pharaoh during Joseph's time. This was called both the land of Rameses and the land of Goshen. This was where the great population of Hebrews lived. We are told in Genesis 47:11:

> Joseph placed his father and his brethren, and gave them a possession in the land of Egypt, in the best of the land, in the land of Rameses, as Pharaoh had commanded.
>
> —KJV

Then in Genesis 47:27 we read:

> Israel dwelt in the land of Egypt, in the country of Goshen; and they had possessions therein, and grew, and multiplied exceedingly.
>
> —KJV

Rameses could not be referring to a city for the simple reason that there just wasn't a city in ancient Egypt large enough to hold the two to three million people Moses led from Egypt, much less all of their flocks and herds. But the Bible says that they were in their homes.

They had to be in their homes! We know that the "angel of death" took the lives of all the firstborn of Egypt, and Pharaoh told Moses to take the people and go! They would have to have been ready when the command came.

Succoth

The area of Succoth (also known as Tharu) is also located near the Delta, or Rameses, where the Israelites were living, and Tharu was where the Egyptian army assembled in preparation for their military expeditions to the north. Armies consisted of a great deal of men, horses, and chariots. They required a large area to assemble properly.

Moses well knew Tharu, called Succoth in the biblical account, and it was here that he organized the people for their journey. This is important to understand primarily because of what happens next. Because if we view the location of Goshen, or Tharu, on a map, it is easy to see that if we just head due east and then turn due south when we reach Arabia, we run directly into the land of Midian. It should have been an easy route.

Succoth to Etham to Pi Hahiroth

Exodus 13:20 tells us that when the Israelites began their journey from Succoth, they "encamped in Etham, in the edge of the wilderness" (KJV). Just before arriving in Etham, I imagine, spirits were still high. Though the route had not taken them due east, as Moses would surely have known was the easiest, it was not a hard trek. With ocean views on one side and picturesque mountains on the other and the sweet taste of freedom lingering everywhere, the journeying Hebrews were surely in a state of constant elation. But then came Etham.

Suddenly they were trapped in, with mountains on the side and in front of them, while reports of Pharaoh's army in pursuit came up from behind them. That's when it hit them. This was the wilderness of the Red Sea. This route was often taken by caravans and armies, because it was safer than traveling along the coast where the Philistines were.

Understand that Etham was not a singular location, like a town. It was a designation of the land that lay around the mid-northern edge of the Gulf of Aqaba. It was here in Etham that God told Moses:

> "Speak to the children of Israel, that they turn and camp before Pi Hahiroth, between Migdol and the sea, opposite Baal Zephon; you shall camp before it by the sea. For Pharaoh will say of the children of Israel, 'They are bewildered by the land; the wilderness has closed them in.' Then I will harden

Pharaoh's heart, so that he will pursue them; and I will gain honor over Pharaoh and over all his army, that the Egyptians may know that I am the LORD." And they did so.

—EXODUS 14:2–4

So at Etham, they stopped traveling north and turned inexplicably—except that God told them to do it—south, through a wadi system that must have appeared as an endless maze to them. Hemmed in on the left and the right, they could travel in only one direction, and the only path that the wadi leads to is a tremendously sized beach that would have easily held the millions of Israelites and their flocks and herds. It was here that they were trapped. It was here that God opened the sea before them.

THE MOUNTAIN OF GOD

The final aspect to consider in the mystery of Sinai is the mountain itself. There is in Saudi Arabia the mountain known today as Jabal al-Lawz. The Saudi government has a missile battery at the top of this mountain and forbids exploration. However, a team infiltrated the area and found astounding proofs that this mountain is, in fact, Mount Sinai. I feel that the Saudi government fears Israel's claim to the mountain. They have, so far, refused further excavation.[1]

THE MYSTERY REVEALED

As with most ancient accounts we tend to hear the story over and over, and with familiarity the details get fuzzy. It is important to note the finer details in the account of the Exodus so that we can see God's greater lesson.

First, looking at where the children of Israel started their journey and then where they were destined, we see that the route they went was, in a word, stupid. It made no sense. They "should have" gone due east out of Goshen, heading across the northern portion of the Sinai Peninsula into the southern portion of what is now Israel and then turned due south into what is now Saudi Arabia. This would have been, essentially, a two-direction "straight line" approach to the journey.

Instead, God sent His chosen people immediately south into a wilderness. Ultimately His direction sent them into what seemed like a trap. Impassable mountains to the north and the west, crashing ocean waves to their right, and Pharaoh's army behind them. Death had to seem imminent. At the very least their time of freedom was over.

I have often felt like that. Have you? There have been times in my life when I believed I was following God's direction, only to find myself trapped with no way out and the enemy closing in at my back. Hope was utterly lost.

But much like the Hebrews when they were trapped, I have seen God open the sea and make a way for me; not according to my way but according to His way. The mystery revealed in the Exodus is this: there will be times in your life that hope seems lost and there is no way out. But if you will trust God and wait patiently on Him, He will make a way out of no way and, in providing for your escape, simultaneously create the means for the destruction of your enemy.

Chapter 9

The MYSTERY of the LOST
ARK of the COVENANT

IT WOULD NOT be an exaggeration, I think, to say that most of what the American public, and even the American church, knows about the ark of the covenant comes from their knowledge of the fictional adventures of Indiana Jones. When *Raiders of the Lost Ark* burst on the scene in the summer of 1981, it seemed the world was ready for a different kind of hero and an adventure that had a biblical twist. I confess that the scene in the Well of Souls, when Indy and his friend Sallah lifted the ark from its encasement, filled me with excitement and amazement. I couldn't help but wonder what it would be like to gaze at this sacred relic. My mind drifts even now to the description in Exodus of the holy chest:

> You shall make a mercy seat of pure gold; two and a half cubits shall be its length and a cubit and a half its width. And you shall make two cherubim of gold; of hammered work you shall make them at the two ends of the mercy seat. Make one cherub at one end, and the other cherub at the other end; you shall make the cherubim at the two ends of it of one piece with the mercy seat. And the cherubim shall stretch out their wings above, covering the mercy seat with their wings, and they shall face one another; the faces of the cherubim shall be toward the mercy seat. You shall put the mercy seat on top of the ark, and in the ark you shall put the Testimony that I will give you. And there I will meet with you, and I will speak with you from above the mercy seat, from between the two

cherubim which are on the ark of the Testimony, about everything which I will give you in commandment to the children
of Israel.

—Exodus 25:17–22

Why this much work put into what is essentially a memory box?
I have discovered over my years of study that the ark is so much
more than simply a repository for Aaron's budded staff, a golden jar
of manna, and the stone tablets of the Ten Commandments.

The Holy of Holies

Without going into any elaborate description of the tabernacle of
Moses, the tabernacle of David, or any of the temples, suffice it to
say that the plan for these structures was important, and every
piece had meaning. Every section was important and sacred, but
none more so than the dark room hidden behind a four-inch-thick
veil. The ark of the covenant was the only piece of furniture within
the holy of holies. It was made of acacia wood, two and one-half
cubits long, one and one-half cubits broad, and one and one-half
cubits high in its external dimensions, and was plated with gold
inside and out. Running the length of each side was a gold border
extending above the top of the ark so as to keep the lid from moving.
This lid was called the mercy seat. This piece was the size of the ark
and was itself made from acacia wood covered in pure gold.

Upon the lid of the ark, or the mercy seat, at its ends, were
placed the cherubim. Some say that these figures, made out of
beaten gold, resembled humans, with the exception of their wings,
while some authorities think these figures might have been of the
same complex form as the cherubim mentioned by Ezekiel. (See
Ezekiel 1:5–14.) They were probably the same height as a man and
stood facing each other, looking down upon the mercy seat, with
their wings forward. The golden censer, with which the high priest
once a year entered the most holy place, was set upon this lid.

Between the cherubim rested the Shekinah, the cloud in which

Jehovah appeared above the mercy seat. It was not the cloud of incense but the manifest appearance of the divine glory. Because Jehovah manifested His essential presence in this cloud, not only could no unclean and sinful man go before the mercy seat (i.e., approach the holiness of the all-holy God), but even the anointed high priest, if he went before it at his own pleasure or without the expiatory blood of sacrifice, would expose himself to certain death.

THE CONTENTS

The ark contained a golden jar of miraculously preserved manna (Exod. 16:33–34); Aaron's staff that budded (Num. 17:10); the two tables of stone on which Jehovah wrote the Ten Commandments, or rather those prepared by Moses from the original ones, which had been broken by him when he heard of Israel's idolatry (Exod. 40:20); and a copy of the law written by Moses (presumed by some to be the full Pentateuch; Exod. 25:21). This copy of the law is thought to be the same as was afterward discovered in the time of Josiah (2 Kings 22:8). At any rate the law must have been removed—with the other contents—at some point, because in the days of Solomon the ark contained the two tablets only.

First, it is important to understand what the role of the ark was in the day-to-day life of the Israelites.

Most significantly the ark guided the nation. We read in Numbers 10:33–34:

> So they departed from the mountain of the Lord on a journey
> of three days; and the ark of the covenant of the Lord went
> before them for the three days' journey, to search out a resting
> place for them. And the cloud of the Lord was above them by
> day when they went out from the camp.

Not a move was made without putting the Lord first and going where He led. This is important for us today. Far too often we follow the path that seems easiest or safest, but it may not be the path that God wants us to follow.

Additionally the ark established the ground of meeting for God. In Exodus 25:21–22 God said:

> You shall put the mercy seat on top of the ark, and in the ark you shall put the Testimony that I will give you. And there I will meet with you, and I will speak with you from above the mercy seat, from between the two cherubim which are on the ark of the Testimony, about everything which I will give you in commandment to the children of Israel.

It is important to note that God wants to meet with us as He sits in His mercy seat. He will always deal with us from a place of mercy, but we have to meet Him in the place and manner in which He says to meet with Him, not necessarily in the place or in the way that we would most like.

So it is plain to see that the ark of the covenant was a very important item, if not the most important item, in the inventory of Israel. What would the Israelites do if the unthinkable happened?

THE ARK DISAPPEARS

He was a mere eight years of age when he ascended to the throne, but he was blessed with a mother, Jedidah, and advisers who helped the young king, Josiah, to make the right decisions. We are told that Josiah "did what was right in the eyes of the Lord and followed completely the ways of his father David,[1] not turning aside to the right or to the left." According to the chronicle of his reign, Josiah began earnestly seeking God at the age of sixteen, and at the age of twenty he became so enraged at the idolatry in his country that he purged the land of all the "high places" of the pagan gods.

His expansion of reforms spread through the areas of Manasseh, Ephraim, and as far north as Naphtali. At the tender age of twenty-six Josiah began rebuilding the temple. As funds poured in from the north and south, they were given to the priests and Levites to complete the needed repairs. It was during this period that Hilkiah, the high priest, found hidden in the temple the Book of the Law that had been given through Moses. (See 2 Chronicles 34:15.) Hilkiah gave the book to Shaphan, the king's scribe, who in turn read the words to King Josiah.

When Josiah heard the words of the law, he tore his robes in despair, for it was then that he realized how far afoul the land had gone in obeying God's commands. He sent the high priest and others to the prophetess Huldah, who confirmed the veracity of what they had found. Josiah read the entire book to all the elders of Judah and Jerusalem. He renewed the covenant and called on the citizens to pledge their faithfulness to it. Josiah provided thirty thousand sheep and thirty thousand cattle for Passover. It was the first time that the feast had been celebrated in that colossal a fashion since the time of the prophet Samuel.

And now we come to the part of the story that bears special significance for our purposes. In 2 Chronicles 35:3 we read:

> Then [Josiah] said to the Levites who taught all Israel, who were holy to the LORD: "Put the holy ark in the house which Solomon the son of David, king of Israel, built. It shall no longer be a burden on your shoulders. Now serve the LORD your God and His people Israel."

This occurred about 621 BC, just thirty-five years before the destruction of Jerusalem and the temple by Nebuchadnezzar, when Judah went into the second phase of their Babylonian captivity. This is significant, because later a very detailed account was given of the items taken to Babylon from both the king's house and the house of the Lord. How detailed? Items as large as bronze pillars and as small as spoons are mentioned in the list found in 2 Kings 25:13–17. But the ark is nowhere mentioned in any of these lists, nor is it listed in any of the items returned. Since we are told in

Jeremiah 28:3 that the Lord had said He would bring back "all the vessels of the LORD's house, that Nebuchadnezzar, king of Babylon, took away from this place and carried to Babylon," we must therefore concluded that the ark was neither taken from nor, obviously, returned to Jerusalem.

THE ARK HIDDEN

The ark must have been hidden sometime in the period between the eighteenth year of Josiah's reign (this is when we are told that he had it taken to Solomon's temple) and thirty-five years later, when the temple was destroyed. As already mentioned, we know it was not taken to Babylon. We are left to conclude from the evidence, then, that at some point during Josiah's reign the ark was taken from the holy of holies and hidden, probably to protect it from the invading hordes of the Babylonians. But is there any evidence to support this directly?

A striking Hebrew tradition exists as to the ark of the covenant. Specifically we find in the Apocryphal book of 2 Maccabees (2:4–8) that the ark was taken by the prophet Jeremiah and secreted in a cavern at the time of the Babylonian capture of the city and that its hiding place has never been found, and never will be, until the Messiah shall set up His kingdom and restore the glory of Israel. Read the passage found in 2 Maccabees:

> It was also in the writing that the prophet [Jeremiah], having received an oracle, ordered that the tent and the ark should follow with him, and that he went out to the mountain where Moses had gone up and had seen the inheritance of God. And Jeremiah came and found a cave, and he brought there the tent and the ark and the altar of incense, and he sealed up the entrance. Some of those who followed him came up to mark the way, but could not find it. When Jeremiah learned of it, he rebuked them and declared: "The place shall be unknown until God gathers his people together again and shows his

mercy. And then the Lord will disclose these things, and the glory of the Lord and the cloud will appear, as they were shown in the case of Moses, and as Solomon asked that the place should be specially consecrated."

—2 MACCABES 2:4–8, RSV

It is important to note that the lines above could have been mistranslated and could have originally stated that the ark was not placed in the mountain Moses was *on* when he viewed the Promised Land (remember that Moses did not enter the Promised Land with the children of Israel) but that the ark was, instead, placed in the mountain that Moses *saw* when he viewed the Promised Land. From Nebo Moses could have seen Jerusalem because of its altitude.

In the pseudepigraphical book *Paralipomena of Jeremiah* (meaning "the remaining words of Jeremiah"), it is also recorded that Jeremiah, in obedience to God's command, hid the sacred objects from the temple just before the destruction of Jerusalem. Now neither of these books are to be trusted as holy writ; however, they show a strong tradition of Jeremiah hiding, or having someone else hide, the ark and other objects from the temple. Is there any truth in these stories? It seems to me to be more than plausible, as Jeremiah was the prophet in Jerusalem during the time of Josiah (when the ark was brought back into the temple), and he continued through the time of the destruction of Jerusalem. It is logical to believe that God directed him to have the ark and other sacred items hidden.

But we come back to the question of scriptural validation. Is there anything in the Bible that supports even the idea of Jeremiah, or someone, secreting the ark away? Read the words of Jeremiah 3:16, where the Lord says:

> "Then it shall come to pass, when you are multiplied and increased in the land in those days," says the LORD, "that they will say no more, 'The ark of the covenant of the LORD.' It

shall not come to mind, nor shall they remember it, nor shall they visit it, nor shall it be made anymore."

This passage indicates that Jeremiah did, in fact, have knowledge that the Israelites would no longer have the ark when they returned from Babylon. It is also important to note the Lord clearly indicated, "Neither shall [that be done] *any more*" (Jer. 3:17, KJV, emphasis added). This is proof that there is no promise of the ark ever being reinstated. In fact, later in Ezekiel, when instructions are given for the temple, there are no instructions given that include even a mention of the ark. It is never mentioned.

THE LOST ARK

Mount Moriah is mentioned only twice in the Bible. We first read about it in the sobering account of Abraham's instruction to sacrifice Isaac. We read in Genesis 22:2 that the Lord told Abraham:

> Take now your son, your only son Isaac, whom you love, and go to the land of Moriah, and offer him there as a burnt offering on one of the mountains of which I shall tell you.

Later we read in 2 Chronicles 3:1:

> Solomon began to build the house of the LORD at Jerusalem on Mount Moriah, where the LORD had appeared to his father David, at the place that David had prepared on the threshing floor of Ornan the Jebusite.

This is important because we have to remember that Jerusalem was situated on two giant hills commonly referred to as Mount Moriah and Mount Zion. Moriah is to the east, while Zion is to the west (and the Mount of Olives is farther east yet than Moriah). The valleys on the eastern, southern, and western sides naturally protected Jerusalem, but the northern area of Mount Moriah was a weak point strategically. To abate this failing, a kind of dry moat was quarried out of the northern portion of Mount Moriah. This quarry prevented an enemy from having the ability to breach the city walls from that direction. At some point this portion of Moriah was used as a stone quarry, and this lowered the ground level to that of the trench that extends just outside the northern wall. This created a cliff face immediately recognizable to visitors of the Holy Land and well known to readers of the Bible: for this area created the Calvary escarpment that contains the skull face that many believe was Golgotha. Importantly for our discussion, it also contains the area known as Jeremiah's Grotto, or Gordon's Calvary.

In January of 1979 Ron Wyatt began excavating in this area. He and his team began by digging straight down along the cliff face. Their first discovery was the appearance of shelf-like niches cut into the face of the cliff. As they dug farther down, they discovered three of these niches with a smaller recess to the right. Ron became convinced that these were cut into the cliff face to hold signs or notices.[2]

It is easy, though, to write history onto things we find, but consider the words of Quintilian, the noted Roman rhetorician:

> Whenever we crucify criminals, very crowded highways are chosen, so that many shall see it and may be moved by fear of it, because all punishment does not pertain so much to revenge as to example.[3]

Three elements typified the Roman crucifixion, and they are recounted in the Gospels. First, there was a public scourging, the severity of which was somewhat arbitrary. Second, there was the public scorn heaped on the individual as he carried his cross (or crossbeam) to the site of execution, where the victim was nailed or bound to the crossbeam, which was then attached to the upright post. The final element, which fits in with Quintilian's description of the purpose of this method of execution, was the signage. In order to deter other would-be criminals (or criminals yet uncaught), the crime of the victim had to be posted clearly for the benefit of viewers or passersby. (Remember that it was possible for a person to last days on a cross, and often the body was left to rot away along the roads and highways. Recall the carnage of Spartacus and his 6,600-plus followers crucified along the length of Rome's Appian Way.)

While interesting to Wyatt, these niches were not the purpose of his dig. Wyatt was looking for the ark of the covenant. As the excavation continued, the team found many articles of interest, but it was when Wyatt found a rock covered in travertine that he began to get excited. This rock was found covering a twelve- to thirteen-inch square hole cut into the bedrock. Wyatt deduced that this hole had held the cross on which Jesus was crucified. There was in this hole a crack that appeared to have been caused by an earthquake. The shaft of the hole reached twenty-three and a half inches into the bedrock, but the crack seemed to extend much farther down. It would be more than a year later before he learned that the crack extended more than twenty feet down through the rock.[4]

THE ARK...FOUND?

As the team continued to clear the area outward from the cliff face, the layout of a building was found. One wall ran parallel to the cliff, along the top of an elevated platform section of bedrock. Two exterior walls extended out at ninety-degree angles from each end of the wall. As the dig continued, Wyatt's team found a great stone that, when measured using subsurface interface radar from above ground, measured over thirteen feet in diameter. In this area, directly below the supposed cross hole previously mentioned, was a system of caves that Wyatt explored for two years.[5]

What concerns us now is the day that Wyatt, led by an Arab guide, went into a particular cave. There before them was an opening of approximately eighteen inches. Wyatt's guide crawled through with a flashlight but soon came out, terrified, and never returned to the site.[6] Wyatt entered and made the greatest discovery yet discussed in this book.

At 2:00 p.m. on Wednesday, January 6, 1982, with only eighteen inches worth of clearance, Wyatt crawled into the opening. Expectant because of what had happened to his guide "James," Wyatt shone his light down through the massive pile of large rock, and his eye caught a glimpse of something reflective. He began slowly removing rocks one at a time and discovered some dry-rotted wooden timbers just beneath the rocks, as well as some rotted animal skins that turned to powder at his touch. The skins were covering a gold veneered table with a raised molding around the side, which consisted of an alternating pattern of a bell and a pomegranate. It only took him a moment to realize that this was, at the very least, an object from the first temple. He was unable to uncover the entire table, but after closer examination and further research, he concluded that this was probably the table of showbread.[7]

But it was the next discovery that would change his life forever. Wyatt shone the beam from his flashlight around and discovered a crack in the ceiling. The crack was covered with a black substance. His mind immediately returned to the cross hole above him. It too had been covered in a shiny black substance. Crawling his way toward the cracked area, he noticed that beneath this area was another stone case extending through the rocks. The lid of the case had cracked completely in two, and the smaller portion had moved away, creating an opening to the interior of the case. The top, Ron recalls, was too close to the top of the cave for him to clearly see inside, yet he knew what was inside the stone case. The crack in the ceiling was directly above the cracked and open portion of the lid, and the black substance had fallen from the crack into the case. Wyatt said he could see vestiges of it on the portion of lid that remained. It was at this time, as Wyatt recalls, as the realization of what had happened there dawned on him, that he passed out.[8] (Note: Disclaimer at the end of this chapter.)

THE MYSTERY REVEALED

What had happened there was that from the base of Jesus's cross, the twenty-three-inch hole where the cross had been situated, the blood of Jesus had collected, and when the great earthquake occurred, the crack broke through the bedrock and split the lid of the stone casing, allowing the blood of God's precious Lamb to flow through the layers of rock and fall onto the mercy seat of the ark of the covenant.

You see, in ancient Israel the high priest collected the blood of the sacrificial lamb and poured it over the mercy seat. This was a shadow that God fulfilled during the crucifixion of Jesus. Ron Wyatt claimed that he had discovered physical proof of the fulfillment of this prophecy. He maintained to have later verified the presence of the ark by use of a colonoscope. However, he reported that the authorities stopped the reporting of the discovery, have withheld evidence, and have sealed off the area from further exploration.

Why would God reveal this ark today, after all this time, especially after Christ has already become the once and eternal sacrifice? The answer can only be found through the study of "types" of the earthly sacrificial system.

What is important for us to remember is that during the time of the tabernacle and the temple, a prescribed ritual took place for the atonement of sins and that, without this, no forgiveness, no right standing, could be found with God. Specifically the blood of the sacrificial lamb was collected in a special basin. This basin was carried by the high priest into the holy of holies, where the high priest remained in pitch darkness for a period of three hours. The high priest then prayed to God for His forgiveness of the sins of the people. The blood in the basin was then poured onto the mercy seat. The Shekinah glory appeared between the cherubim over the mercy seat. This demonstrated God's forgiveness of the people's sin. The high priest then stood and cried out, "It is finished." (See Leviticus 16:1–28.)

Jesus is declared in various places in the New Testament to be our High Priest. The entire ceremony detailed above is described in the New Testament. Additionally in Jeremiah 31:31 God declared, "Behold, the days are coming, says the Lord, when I will make a new covenant with the house of Israel." And finally in the Book of Daniel we read that the angel Gabriel appeared to Daniel to give him help in understanding the vision that he, Daniel, had had. Gabriel said:

> Seventy weeks are determined for your people and for your holy city, to finish the transgression, to make an end of sins, to make reconciliation for iniquity, to bring in everlasting righteousness, to seal up vision and prophecy, and to anoint the Most Holy.
>
> —Daniel 9:24

This is a prophecy of the work of Messiah—a work that would culminate in the ultimate anointing of the Most Holy, or, as has been discussed, that place that was most holy in the eyes of Israel, the mercy seat.

This is represented in John's vision of the opening of the temple of God in heaven, into the throne room of God:

> Then the temple of God was opened in heaven, and the ark of His covenant was seen in His temple. And there were lightnings, noises, thunderings, an earthquake, and great hail.
>
> —Revelation 11:19

Again in Revelation there is an account of the opening of God's throne room, but here we learn what occurs after this, when Christ is finished with His great final act of atonement:

> After these things I looked, and behold, the temple of the tabernacle of the testimony in heaven was opened. And out of the temple came the seven angels having the seven plagues, clothed in pure bright linen, and having their chests girded

with golden bands. Then one of the four living creatures gave to the seven angels seven golden bowls full of the wrath of God who lives forever and ever. The temple was filled with smoke from the glory of God and from His power, and no one was able to enter the temple till the seven plagues of the seven angels were completed.

—REVELATION 15:5–8

What John witnessed was the completion of the antitypical Day of Atonement, which was foreshadowed in the typical on earth. As we read of the earthly Day of Atonement of the sacrificial system, we see the similarities between the two when we compare the verses.

In Revelation 15:8 we read that "the temple was filled with smoke," and in Leviticus 16:13 we read that the high priest "shall put the incense on the fire before the LORD, that the cloud of incense may cover the mercy seat that is on the Testimony, lest he die." Then later in Revelation 15:8 we read, "And no one was able to enter the temple." And in Leviticus 16:17 we read, "There shall be no man in the tabernacle of meeting when he goes in to make atonement in the Holy Place, until he comes out, that he may make atonement for himself, for his household, and for all the assembly of Israel."

So there is in heaven a mirror of what has happened on earth. Read the staggering words in 1 John 5:7:

> For there are three that bear witness in heaven: the Father, the Word, and the Holy Spirit; and these three are one.

Yes, there are witnesses in heaven who bear out the truth of God's grace found in the blood of Jesus. When we are covered in the blood, we are *His*! But John does not stop there! In verse 7 John tells of the three heavenly witnesses, but in verse 8 he reminds us:

> There are three that bear witness on earth: the Spirit, *the water*, and *the blood*; and these three agree as one.

—EMPHASIS ADDED

The mystery revealed is simply this: as God instructed the high priest to pour out the blood onto the mercy seat, and as God divinely ordered that the blood of Jesus flow down through the rocks of Calvary onto the mercy seat, so has He ordered that the blood of Jesus, God's precious, perfect Lamb, be applied over your heart and your life. The witness of the Spirit in your life, the witness of the water, and the witness of the blood "agree as one" so that when Satan comes to tempt, to mock, or attack you, you can shout with boldness that the blood that was poured out at Calvary has washed over you, and you walk not in a victory you have won but in the ultimate, complete, and final victory that Christ won when He willingly shed His blood, poured it over the mercy seat, and cried "It is finished!" The revealed mystery of the ark of the covenant, dear friend, is that the Spirit, the water, and the blood testify that you walk in victory!

DISCLAIMER: It is important to note, and it would be careless to omit the fact, that subsequent exploration of the garden tomb by those in charge of the Wyatt legacy have not found the opening or room Wyatt claimed to have found. It is possible that they missed it, that it has been filled in and artifacts removed, or that Wyatt simply had a vision.

Chapter 10

The MYSTERY *of the* PRAYER SHAWL

Y EARS SHE SPENT in loneliness. The law forbade any contact
with her. She relied on the kindness of strangers to help her
with the most basic of chores, such as collecting water at the
well. After all, she couldn't go herself. If she so much as touched the
stones of the well wall, the entire thing would be deemed unclean.
No other woman could spend much time with her for fear of
becoming contaminated. No man wanted to be with her. She could
not even find respite in God, for she was forbidden from entering
the local place of worship. Twelve long and lonely years she spent in
that open solitude.

You have probably heard her story recounted in the eighth
chapter of Luke's Gospel, but I wonder how often we think about
her as more than the woman with an issue of blood. It is certainly
hard for us to understand her situation. We are not under Mosaic
Law—and indeed we have virtually tossed out the need of knowing,
much less understanding, this code. But it is important, before we
begin to discuss this next mystery, to understand this woman, the
world she lived in, and the pain—physical, mental, and emotional—
she experienced.

You see, under Mosaic Law, a woman with any issue of blood,
be it menstrual or postpartum bleeding, was to be "put apart" for
a period of seven days. During this time anything she lay on or sat
on was considered unclean. Understand that this meant if she sat
on a blanket and then you touched the blanket (even if you didn't
touch a part that was bloodied), you had to go through a ritual

cleansing of your clothes and body to become clean again. If a man was sexually intimate with her during this time, he shared in her uncleanness and was himself "put apart" for a period of seven days.

Now the woman mentioned above had experienced this issue of blood for twelve years. Again, according to the law, all of her days were considered unclean. Accordingly *she* was to be considered and treated as unclean. Because of this she would had to have lived a life "put apart" from her community for the duration of those twelve years. Had she been married, her husband would have had to divorce her. She would have been unable to care for or even see her children. She would have been unable to seek solace in her house of worship or even be visited by her local rabbi.

Now consider her physical state. This woman had been bleeding for *twelve years*! If you have ever been stricken with any kind of anemia, you know how taxing that can be on the body. This woman probably suffered from menorrhagia, which is an abnormally heavy and long menstruation that is accompanied by severe cramping and inordinate blood loss. Consequently normal daily activities would have been virtually impossible. The blood loss is substantial—the Scriptures refer to it as a hemorrhage—to the point of being able to fill a sanitary napkin every couple of hours. And this woman dealt with this for twelve years! According to the US National Library of Medicine, there are several possible causes of menorrhagia, such as:

- Endometrial hyperplasia
- Von Willebrand disease and other bleeding disorders
- Uterine polyps
- Ovarian cysts
- Glandular issues resulting in severe hormonal changes
- Thyroid malfunction
- Clotting disorders

- Uterine fibroids

- Cancer

The least of these, in my opinion (hormonal imbalances caused by glandular issues), would still be a horrible thing to face, and this poor woman dealt with it for more than a decade! The Scriptures say that this woman spent all that she had on physicians, and not only could they not help her, but she, in fact, grew worse. Today menorrhagia is treatable with hormone pills but often is only curable via hysterectomy (a removal of the uterus) or endometrial ablation or resection (a process that permanently destroys the uterine lining). Now that we have a better sense of the woman, let's revisit her story.

THE TABERNACLE

Jairus, the leader of the local synagogue, had come to search out Jesus. His little daughter, only twelve years old, lay dying back at his house. Jairus begged Jesus to come and heal her. As they set out, the people of the town pressed in around Jesus. When suddenly:

> A woman, having a flow of blood for twelve years, who had spent all her livelihood on physicians and could not be healed by any, came from behind and touched the border of His garment. And immediately her flow of blood stopped.
> And Jesus said, "Who touched Me?"
> When all denied it, Peter and those with him said, "Master, the multitudes throng and press You, and You say, 'Who touched Me?'"
> But Jesus said, "Somebody touched Me, for I perceived power going out from Me." Now when the woman saw that she was not hidden, she came trembling; and falling down before Him, she declared to Him in the presence of all the people the reason she had touched Him and how she was healed immediately.

> And He said to her, "Daughter, be of good cheer; your faith
> has made you well. Go in peace."
>
> —LUKE 8:43–48

People often teach that the "hem" of Jesus's garment was literally just the place where the fabric was sown at the bottom to prevent fraying or that it just referred to the edge of His clothing. There is nothing wrong with this understanding, per se. After all, Jesus Himself said that it was the woman's faith that made her well. But is there more to understand about this story?

In the Book of Numbers we read an instruction given to Moses by the Lord:

> Again the LORD spoke to Moses, saying, "Speak to the children of Israel: Tell them to make tassels on the corners of their garments throughout their generations, and to put a blue thread in the tassels of the corners. And you shall have the tassel, that you may look upon it and remember all the commandments of the LORD and do them, and that you may not follow the harlotry to which your own heart and your own eyes are inclined, and that you may remember and do all My commandments, and be holy for your God. I am the LORD your God, who brought you out of the land of Egypt, to be your God: I am the LORD your God."
>
> —NUMBERS 15:37–41

Later in Deuteronomy we read a similar instruction:

> You shall make tassels on the four corners of the clothing with which you cover yourself.
>
> —DEUTERONOMY 22:12

The garment described here is called a *tallit*. It is, at its simplest, a prayer shawl. It is rectangular, and each corner has tassels knotted together called *tzitzits*. The word *tallit* is actually a compound Hebrew word from the words *tal* meaning "tent" and *ith* meaning "little." The prayer shawl, then, is intended by God to be a "little tent" or "little tabernacle" for the individual. Recall Jesus's instruction given in Matthew 6:6, where He said:

> When you pray, go into your room, and when you have shut your door, pray to your Father who is in the secret place; and your Father who sees in secret will reward you openly.

The tallit is meant to be a personal tent of meeting—a secret place of prayer and intimacy with God.

A brief description

It is necessary before proceeding to give those of you who may have never seen this garment a description of it, for its craftsmanship is important to its understanding.

The tallit has an inscribed band around the neck. It reads (as translated), "Blessed are You, Lord our God, King of the universe, who has sanctified us with His commandments and commanded us regarding the commandment of fringes (tzitzits)." This is important, because it acknowledges that the "little tent" the tallit's wearer is entering is one that has been ordained by God. This is the banded area that you kiss prior to putting on the tallit. This alludes to the fact that the powerful (effectual, fervent) prayer is one that is based on worship. The Greek word for worship is *proskuneō*, which means to "kiss toward."

The materials of the tallit are varied, but traditional tallit are made entirely of wool. This, of course, represents the blood of the sacrifices, the laws, its protection, and covering.

Finally we must pay some special attention to the tzitzits. These easily dismissible fringes are pregnant with meaning and symbolism. First of all, it is important to remember that every letter of the Hebrew alphabet has a numerical value. This is not numerology as we know it today but was used to denote special meaning to words. In the letters of the word צִיצִת (tzitzits) in Hebrew, the value is 600. Each fringe, or tzitzit, is comprised of eight cords and five knots.

This makes a total of 613. There are 613 commandments in the law of Moses (365 prohibitions and 248 affirmations). Additionally the unspoken name of God, יְהֹוָה or YHVH (Jehovah), can be found in the tzitzits. The name in Hebrew is made up of the letters *yod*, *hey*, *vav*, and *hey*. These are the tenth, fifth, sixth, and fifth letters of the alphabet. The tzitzit is tied with a knot and ten windings, another knot and five windings, another knot and six windings, and a final knot with five windings. Interestingly, in the Ashkenazi tradition, the tzitzits are tied a little differently but still point to God. Specifically each tzitzit is tied with thirty-nine total windings. The first knot is followed by seven windings, the second knot by eight windings, the third by eleven windings, and the fourth by thirteen windings. The sum of the first three is twenty-six, the numerical value of YHVH, and the final number, thirteen, is the numerical value of *echad*, or "One." This is the foundational faith known as the "Shema," which states, "Hear, O Israel, the Lord Your God, the Lord is one." The final phrase "The Lord is one" is, in Hebrew, *YHVH echad*.

The tallit in relationships

The tallit is an indispensible item in Jewish weddings. Often the bride will present her groom with a tallit, which he will wrap around himself. Also, the tallit can be placed over the head of both bride and groom together during the recitation of the Sheva Brachot (the seven blessings). Finally, the wedding canopy itself is often made of a full-size tallit (called a *tallit gadol*).

In Genesis 2:24 we read:

> Therefore a man shall leave his father and mother and be joined to his wife, and they shall become one flesh.

The covering of the two, the bride and groom, beautifully represents this truth as they come under the covering of God as one flesh.

Ruth

Nowhere, I think, in the entirety of Scripture is the use of the tallit and its symbolism in relationship better displayed than in the story of Ruth. Recall that Ruth was Naomi's daughter-in-law and that Ruth's husband, brother-in-law, and father-in-law had all died. Naomi then decided to return home to Judah. Naomi's first daughter-in-law, Orpah, returned to her own family and "to her gods" (Ruth 1:15), and Naomi encouraged Ruth to do the same. But Ruth steadfastly refused, and so returned to Judah with Naomi.

In an effort to support herself and her mother-in-law, Ruth gleaned the four corners of the fields (as was the custom of the indigent in those days) of Naomi's kinsman Boaz. Upon seeing her diligently working, Boaz gave special instructions that none of his men were to approach her and that she should have special concessions in taking water from his wells. When he told her all of this, Ruth fell at his feet and asked how she could possibly have found such favor in his sight. Boaz replied:

> It has been fully reported to me, all that you have done for your mother-in-law since the death of your husband, and how you have left your father and your mother and the land of your birth, and have come to a people whom you did not know before. The LORD repay your work, and a full reward be given you by the LORD God of Israel, under whose wings you have come for refuge.
>
> —RUTH 2:11–12

This phrase "under whose wings you have come" is the same phrase used in the prophecy of Malachi, in which he said:

> "For behold, the day is coming, burning like an oven, and all the proud, yes, all who do wickedly will be stubble. And the day which is coming shall burn them up," says the LORD of hosts, "that will leave them neither root nor branch. But to

you who fear My name the Sun of Righteousness shall arise with healing in His wings."

—Malachi 4:1–2

The Hebrew word for "wings" in this passage is *kanaf*, which has a very specific definition. It literally means the very fringes of the feathers of a bird. It did not mean the entire wing, just the fringes. Now back to Ruth.

Where this phrase becomes important is later in Ruth's story. Ruth reported to Naomi what Boaz had done and the favor he had shown her. Naomi told Ruth to wash and anoint herself, put on her best garment, and go that night to where Boaz was winnowing barley at the threshing floor. You see, Boaz was a kinsman of Naomi's and, therefore, had a right and an obligation to choose to care for Ruth (and, by extension, Naomi) by taking Ruth as his wife.

Naomi instructed Ruth, "Do not make yourself known to the man until he has finished eating and drinking. Then it shall be, when he lies down, that you shall notice the place where he lies; and you shall go in, uncover his feet, and lie down; and he will tell you what you should do" (Ruth 3:3–4).

So Ruth put on her best outfit and dolled herself up and went to where Boaz was working. After Boaz had eaten his dinner and "his heart was cheerful" (v. 7), he lay himself down at the end of a heap of grain. Ruth stole quietly in, uncovered Boaz's feet, and lay down near him.

Hours later Boaz was startled awake and, the Bible says, turned himself and found a woman lying at his feet. "Who are you?" he asked. And Ruth answered him, saying, "I am Ruth, your maidservant. Take your maidservant under your wing, for you are a close relative" (v. 9).

Be clear here. There was no sexual impropriety happening in this relationship. Ruth went in and humbly sought protection under Boaz's covering—the protection found under his wing. When she said to him, "You are a close relative," she was, essentially, saying,

"You know my situation. You know that I am alone in this world with Naomi, my mother-in-law, and I cannot protect us. Will you take me as your wife and be my covering of protection?"

The Bible records that Boaz responded to her by saying:

> Blessed are you of the LORD, my daughter! For you have shown more kindness at the end than at the beginning, in that you did not go after young men, whether poor or rich. And now, my daughter, do not fear. I will do for you all that you request, for all the people of my town know that you are a virtuous woman. Now it is true that I am a close relative; however, there is a relative closer than I. Stay this night, and in the morning it shall be that if he will perform the duty of a close relative for you—good; let him do it. But if he does not want to perform the duty for you, then I will perform the duty for you, as the LORD lives! Lie down until morning.
>
> —RUTH 3:10–13

Boaz acknowledged and affirmed her again and then said that he would care for her.

The cloth that Boaz was covered with was his tallit. When Ruth uncovered his feet and then covered herself, she was placing herself under the fringes of his tallit!

AUTHORITY

I don't have space here to look too much further in depth at all the layers and symbols inherent in the tallit, but I would be remiss if I did not discuss this most important aspect. You see, while it is true that the tallit also represents the Shekinah glory of God, and it serves as a reminder to us of the names of God and the promises of God, it is important to note that the color blue is prevalent in the tallit.

Now for us living in the Western world in the twenty-first century, that means nothing. I have multiple blue button-down shirts, blue T-shirts, blue slacks, blue jeans, blue socks, blue ties; I also have a few purple shirts, purple ties, etc. You get the idea. But in ancient times blue was a remarkably difficult color to produce. There is a reason that we call a certain shade royal blue. Purple was difficult to make as well, because after all, purple cannot be made without blue and red mixed together. Only royalty could wear these colors, because they were so expensive to produce. In fact, in 200 BC one pound of cloth dyed blue cost the equivalent of $36,000, and by AD 300 the cost had risen to an equivalent of $96,000. Therefore, when Luke describes Lydia in Acts 16:14 as a "seller of purple," he is making a very conspicuous statement. He is saying that Lydia, a recent convert, was also one of the wealthiest people in the empire.

At any rate, the reason this is important for us is because blue is the color of authority. When we place ourselves under the tallit, it is a physical representation of entering into that "secret place of the Most High" (Ps. 91:1), but it is also a physical representation of wrapping ourselves in the authority of the royal priesthood into which we were ordained when we asked God to pour the blood of Jesus over our hearts and lives. Under the tallit, under the promises of God, we can stand confident in our authority and sure of our protection under the shadow of His wings.

THE MYSTERY REVEALED

What then is the revelation of the mystery of the tallit? I have already explained that the tallit is a private place of meeting for you and God, that it is the secret place of the Most High, that the tzitzits represent God, His commandments, and His promises, and that the tallit is a physical manifestation of the authority we find in God. There is, however, one thing I have not yet shared. The word *tzitzit* comes from a root that means "to gaze upon." When we enter the covering of the tallit, we enter a place where we can gaze upon the promises of God. What are the promises of God?

In Exodus 19 God reminded the Israelites and, by extension, us:

> You have seen what I did to the Egyptians, and how I bore you
> on eagles' wings and brought you to Myself. Now therefore, if
> you will indeed obey My voice and keep My covenant, then
> you shall be a special treasure to Me above all people; for all
> the earth is Mine.
>
> —EXODUS 19:4–5

In the shadow of His wing we not only experience His deliverance but also our own transformation into a special treasure above all people in God's sight.

In conclusion, now that we have a better understanding of that special covering Jesus wore and of the greater significance of the fringes of His shawl, we can better understand the desperation of that poor woman who suffered with the horrendous disease that resulted in an issuance of blood for twelve years. How frantic she must have been, to risk further social ostracization, to press her "unclean" body through that throng, and in a moment of eager anticipation to cry out, "If only I could touch the fringes of His prayer shawl! If only I could grasp onto Jehovah Rapha, I know I could be made whole!"

How desperate are you? Do you need to reach out and touch Jehovah Rapha, the God who heals you? Perhaps you need a special touch from Jehovah Jireh, the Lord who provides. Or do you need to feel the calming grace of Jehovah Shalom, your Lord of perfect peace? Whatever your need of God is, that special provision can be found in that secret place under the shadow of His wings.

Chapter 11

The MYSTERY *of* HANUKKAH

I N 167 BC Syrian-Greco forces seized the Jewish temple and dedicated it to the worship of the Greek god Zeus. The Jewish people were, understandably, distraught, but fear of governmental retaliation kept them in check. Antiochus Epiphanes, the governor, then made the observance of Judaism a capital offense. Following that, in a move copied directly from Daniel's experience in Babylon, the Jewish people were ordered to worship only Greek gods.[1]

It was in the village of Modi'in that the seeds of revolt began to break through the hardened ground of apathy. It was there that Greek soldiers gathered the villagers and forced them to bow down to an idol. Then, in a move meant to pour salt on the wound, the villagers were forced to eat the flesh of a pig. It was when the soldiers ordered Mattathias, the local high priest, to bow and eat that the unrest began. Not surprisingly Mattathias refused to submit. When a villager stepped forward and offered to participate on Mattathias's behalf, the high priest drew his sword and, in a fit of rage, killed the Greek soldier and the indulgent villager! Mattathias's five sons, along with zealous villagers, armed themselves and killed the rest of the garrison in the village.

Mattathias and his family fled the village to hide in the mountains, and other incited Jews later joined them. Eventually the revolutionaries, who came to be known as Maccabees (or Hasmoneans), were successful in taking back their city and ultimately in regaining control of the temple in Jerusalem. Mattathias, who by this time had died, had ceded leadership of the revolt to his third son, Judah Maccabee (Judah the Hammer). Judah ordered the temple to be cleansed, a new altar to be erected in place of the polluted altar of Zeus, and new holy vessels to be made. When all had been completed and the time of dedication had come, it was discovered that there was only enough olive oil to keep the light of the menorah lit not for the full eight days but for only one day. The priest lit the wick anyway, and the flame burned for eight full days!

THE PECULIAR MENORAH

In the years that followed, this became a major feast in the land of Israel. Because the word *Hanukkah* stems from a word meaning "to dedicate," we find references to this feast translated in many English Bibles, not incorrectly, as the Feast of Dedication. The Jewish people commonly call it "The Festival of Lights," and that is because out of that celebration (which occurs in the winter, before Christmas) came a peculiar menorah. The traditional menorah has seven branches and illuminated the holy place wherein was the table of showbread and the altar of incense. In the New Testament Book of Revelation, the seven branches represent the seven churches of Asia Minor as well as the church across the years. Recall the explanation given in the Book of Revelation:

> The mystery of the seven stars which you saw in My right hand, and the seven golden lampstands: The seven stars are the angels of the seven churches, and the seven lampstands which you saw are the seven churches.
>
> —REVELATION 1:20

The tradition of the nine-branched menorah comes from the eight-day miracle and the ninth mystery candle. Some rabbis believe that seven of the branches represent the traditional menorah while the eighth branch represents new beginnings (which, historically is the meaning of the number eight).

What is this ninth candle? Why the change? To answer those questions, we have to turn our eyes to Jesus.

The Gospel of John

The general consensus of the first four books of the New Testament is that they are four different perspectives of the life of Jesus. In the simplest sense this is true. However, many Christians are unaware that while Matthew, Mark, and Luke (called the Synoptic Gospels) are simply biographical in nature, the Gospel of John is written with a particular intent to emphasize the fact that Jesus was the long-awaited Christ. The Messiah was peculiar to the Jewish people. He had specific requirements due to prophecy. His Jewishness was remarkably important. It is interesting, then, to note that John framed his account of Jesus's ministry around a cycle of Jewish feasts. After John's eloquent opening chapter (which confirms Jesus's identity as the Messiah not only in its own text but also in the account of John the Baptist's verification of Jesus as Messiah), chapter 2 opens with the miracle at the wedding of Cana—which effectively signaled the beginning of Jesus's ministry—and then moves to the Feast of Passover in verse 13. What starts at Passover in chapter 2 continues in chapter 5 at the Feast of Pentecost, on to chapter 7 and the Feast of Tabernacles, and for our purposes, moving on to chapter 10 and the Feast of Dedication, or Hanukkah.

What makes the mention of the Feast of Dedication in John so intriguing are the events of the ninth chapter. At the close of chapter 8 Jesus makes the bold declaration, "Before Abraham was, I AM!" (John 8:58). Then at the opening of chapter 9 we read:

> Now as Jesus passed by, He saw a man who was blind from birth. And His disciples asked Him, saying, "Rabbi, who sinned, this man or his parents, that he was born blind?"
>
> Jesus answered, "Neither this man nor his parents sinned, but that the works of God should be revealed in him. I must

work the works of Him who sent Me while it is day; the night
is coming when no one can work. As long as I am in the world,
I am the light of the world."

In the declaration *prior* to the blind man's healing, Jesus
declared Himself to be *the* light! After this Jesus made the mud,
put it on the man's eyes, had him wash in the Pool of Siloam, and
subsequently, the Bible says, "the man...came home seeing" (John
9:7, NIV).

Now this blind man was well known in his town. We can tell
this from the account, because we read that "his neighbors and
those who had formerly seen him begging asked, 'Isn't this the
same man who used to sit and beg?'" (v. 8, NIV). Some said that it
was, and others said that it was not him. The ambiguity as well as
the curiosity about the identity of the man who healed this blind
beggar led the Pharisees of that area to investigate the situation.

Their investigation, were it not so tragic, would be laughable.
When the Pharisees saw the healed man, they could see—no pun
intended—that this once-blind man (blind from birth, mind you)
had been made whole, and their first observation was that the
healing had been done on the Sabbath. The response from some
of them was not that a healing had been performed, that a miracle
had happened, but that "this man [Jesus] is not from God, for He
does not keep the Sabbath" (v. 16, NIV). Others among them coun-
tered with, "How can a sinner do such miraculous signs?" (v. 16,
NIV). The Bible says they were divided. (As a side note, isn't it sad
that a wonderful miracle could bring such division to ostensibly
pious men?)

Now they asked the man what happened. He told them plainly
what happened. Their response was to ask him more questions.
They turned again to the blind man: "What have you to say about
him? It was your eyes he opened" (v. 17, NIV). The man replied, "He
is a prophet" (v. 17). The Pharisees had asked the man two questions.

He had answered both with fidelity. But you know how it is with the ultra-religious crowd—any answer that rocks the boat is not good enough. So the Pharisees called in the formerly blind man's parents.

Read where the parents are brought in:

> But the Jews did not believe concerning him, that he had been blind and received his sight, until they called the parents of him who had received his sight. And they asked them, saying, "Is this your son, who you say was born blind? How then does he now see?"
>
> —JOHN 9:18–19

Look at that first sentence! This poor man, who should have been out celebrating the fact that he could see after so many years by walking the countryside and looking at flowers, birds, trees, water, etc., was instead enduring interrogation by his church leaders. Though he answered faithfully, his answers ran afoul of their notions and ideas of what and how the miracle should have been done. He was therefore suspect, because after all that, "they still did not believe" (v. 18, NIV) that he had ever been blind in the first place. They went so far as to bring his parents in for questioning. His parents' answers blow the Pharisees' entire argument away. Look at how they respond:

> His parents answered them and said, "We know that this is our son, and that he was born blind; but by what means he now sees we do not know, or who opened his eyes we do not know. He is of age; ask him. He will speak for himself."
>
> —JOHN 9:20–21

The response of these parents affirms their son's earlier affirmations. But look at the real reason they responded this way. In John 9:22–23 we read:

His parents said these things because they feared the Jews, for the Jews had agreed already that if anyone confessed that He was Christ, he would be put out of the synagogue. Therefore his parents said, "He is of age; ask him."

So now, according to Jewish law, the man's testimony as to being blind since birth had been irrevocably affirmed. So the response of the Pharisees was to bring the poor man back in for more questioning.

The Pharisees charged the man, "Give God the glory! We know that [Jesus] is a sinner" (v. 24). Apparently the dissenting Pharisees had been silenced, been removed, or had changed their minds. Their phrase "Give God the glory" is akin to us saying, "Tell the truth, so help you God." Now bear in mind what we just read back in verse 22; confession of Jesus as the Christ was enough to get a person kicked out of the synagogue. That put him out of reach of salvation. What was this poor man to do? It amazes me that God put the exact right words on his lips, for the Bible records him responding to them as follows:

Whether He is a sinner or not I do not know. One thing I know: that though I was blind, now I see.

—JOHN 9:25

And that really should have done it. So the Pharisees questioned him some more.

They said to him, "What did He do to you? How did He open your eyes?" (v. 26). Notice that they were asking questions that had been asked and answered! Where was the quintessential TV lawyer raising an objection? This poor man, left alone by friends and even by his parents, responded by saying:

I told you already, and you did not listen. Why do you want to hear it again? *Do you also* want to become His disciples?

—JOHN 9:27, EMPHASIS ADDED

Those words "do you also" are powerful. This man declared that he was throwing his lot in with the Man who had seen his need and met it, not with the Pharisees who repeatedly questioned and even threatened him. But this phrase was also his undoing, because the Pharisees responded by yelling at the man that they were disciples of Moses, and they didn't even know where Jesus was from. The man rebuked them, and the Pharisees excommunicated him.

Jesus saves.

The story recounts that Jesus heard what happened to this poor man and sought him out. When Jesus found him, He asked a simple question: "Do you believe in the Son of God?" (John 9:35).

Imagine, if you can, the weight on this poor man's shoulders. More questions! But this one does not have the taint of accusation. He responds to Jesus with a question of his own: "Who is He, Lord, that I may believe in Him?" (v. 36).

And Jesus responded to him by saying, "You have both seen Him and it is He who is talking with you" (v. 37). Jesus clearly declared that He is Messiah. Read how the conversation transpired:

> Then [the man] said, "Lord, I believe!" And he worshiped Him.
>
> And Jesus said, "For judgment I have come into this world, that those who do not see may see, and that those who see may be made blind."
>
> Then some of the Pharisees who were with Him heard these words, and said to Him, "Are we blind also?"
>
> Jesus said to them, "If you were blind, you would have no sin; but now you say, 'We see.' Therefore your sin remains."
>
> —John 9:38–41

Now this has been a long setup, but the context is remarkably important. See how Jesus revealed a mystery in John 9:35: "Do you believe in the Son of God?" Jesus then illumined the man's understanding by shining His light on him. All of this leads to the moment in John 10:22–24 at which we are told that as Jesus entered the temple via Solomon's porch during the Feast of Dedication, He was accosted by members of the Jewish community, who demanded of Him, "How long do You keep us in doubt? If You are the Christ, tell us plainly!"

In an echo of the previous chapter's interrogation, Jesus said (and still says today):

> I told you, and you do not believe. The works that I do in My Father's name, they bear witness of Me. But you do not believe, because you are not of My sheep, as I said to you. My sheep hear My voice, and I know them, and they follow Me. And I give them eternal life, and they shall never perish; neither shall anyone snatch them out of My hand. My Father, who has given them to Me, is greater than all; and no one is able to snatch them out of My Father's hand. I and My Father are one.
>
> —JOHN 10:25–30

THE MYSTERY REVEALED

So how does this story relate to Hanukkah? Recall the differences between the traditional seven-branch menorah and the nine-branch menorah of Hanukkah. The menorah (both versions) represents the tree of life. Eight is the number of a new beginning. Jesus brought a new covenant into our understanding by grafting the Gentile people into the Jewish root. That eighth candle represents the new covenant, the new beginning, and the "one new man" church.

But what about the ninth candle?

Let me tell you that the ninth candle is situated higher than the other candles and is the first lit during Hanukkah, and it is this candle that is used to light all the other candles on the subsequent nights. Though the other candles are extinguished after a prescribed amount of time, the ninth candle, the Shamash, traditionally remains lit.

This candle today has come to be called the helper candle. The eight candles represent those lamps that had no oil yet remained lit, while the ninth candle lit the others. This ninth candle is a picture of the Holy Ghost. He is called our Helper. Jesus told the disciples that He was going away but that He would send another. He told them:

> If you love Me, keep My commandments. And I will pray the Father, and He will give you another Helper, that He may abide with you forever—the Spirit of truth, whom the world cannot receive, *because it neither sees Him nor knows Him*; but you know Him, for He dwells with you and will be in you. I will not leave you orphans; I will come to you.
> —JOHN 14:15–18, EMPHASIS ADDED

Now think back to our discussion about the story of the blind man in John 9, and note Jesus's reference to being "the *light* of the world." (I'm not saying that it was intentional, but wouldn't it be just like God to do something like that?)

Why is this important? How is this a mystery revealed? Because Jesus said that the Holy Spirit would come to "teach [us] all things" (John 14:26), would "testify of [Jesus]" (John 15:26), and would "convict the world of sin, and of righteousness, and of judgment" (John 16:8). You see, we are the eight candles! We are oppressed by the enemy. Our bodies, which are God's temple, have been desecrated by sin. We live under siege from the enemy! Yet we have a Helper, a Shamash, a consuming fire! We have the Holy Ghost!

There is a sobering truth recorded in Proverbs 20:27. It reads:

> The spirit of a man is the lamp of the LORD, searching all the inner depths of his heart.

Your spirit, your life, is God's lamp—His candle. Candles need the fire. Candles can only fulfill their purpose with fire. Recall that John told the people gathered at the Jordan that he, John, was not the Messiah, but that the Messiah was greater and that when the Messiah came, they would experience a baptism with the Holy Ghost and with fire!

Oh, how we need that fire. It is time for war on the enemy! It is time to take back our nation, our churches, our families, and our lives. What happens when we light that fire? Read the words of David in Psalm 18:28–42:

> For You will light my lamp; the Lord my God will enlighten my darkness. For by You I can run against a troop, by my God I can leap over a wall. As for God, His way is perfect; the word of the Lord is proven; He is a shield to all who trust in Him.
>
> For who is God, except the Lord? And who is a rock, except our God? It is God who arms me with strength, and makes my way perfect. He makes my feet like the feet of deer, and sets me on my high places. He teaches my hands to make war, so that my arms can bend a bow of bronze.
>
> You have also given me the shield of Your salvation; Your right hand has held me up, Your gentleness has made me great. You enlarged my path under me, so my feet did not slip.
>
> I have pursued my enemies and overtaken them; neither did I turn back again till they were destroyed. I have wounded them, so that they could not rise; they have fallen under my feet. For You have armed me with strength for the battle; You have subdued under me those who rose up against me. You have also given me the necks of my enemies, so that I destroyed those who hated me. They cried out, but there was none to save; even to the Lord, but He did not answer them. Then I beat them as fine as the dust before the wind; I cast them out like dirt in the streets.

It is time to cleanse and purify the temple of our lives and to rededicate them to the service of the Lord. But once that is done, we need the Helper to come and light our lives with His holy fire! For the victory won on Calvary's cross can only be implemented in our day-to-day lives through the fire of the Shamash, our Helper, the fire of the ninth candle!

Chapter 12

The MYSTERY *of* CHRIST

THE FIRST TIME I heard the song "Counting on God" by Jared Anderson, something stirred in me. There was something jarring about the juxtaposition of the words *miracle* and *mystery*. Some would just call it good songwriting, but it brought back to my mind Paul's letter to Timothy, his son in the faith.

Paul desperately wanted to see Timothy, and Paul had every intention to visit him soon. However, Paul was concerned, should he be delayed in making the journey, that Timothy should still receive the instruction that he, Paul, wanted to impart to Timothy. In 1 Timothy 3:15-16 Paul wrote:

> I write so that you may know how you ought to conduct yourself in the house of God, which is the church of the living God, the pillar and ground of the truth. And without controversy great is the mystery of godliness:
> God was manifested in the flesh, justified in the Spirit, seen by angels, preached among the Gentiles, believed on in the world, received up in glory.

We find the noun *mystery* twenty-six times in the New Testament. The apostle Paul uses it twenty-one of those times. This word was brought into our language directly from the Greek word *musterion*. It has as its root a word that means "to close the lips." During Paul's day it was the word used to describe the mystery religion whose secrets were revealed only to devotees who had been initiated. The earliest false cult that Paul battled was a cult that taught that by adhering to their teachings, one could learn deeper secrets. This cult, known as Gnosticism, believed that salvation came through more and more experiential knowledge.

The Mystery Machine

Paul battled the forerunner of this cult in Corinth. This is why the church at Corinth so desperately sought the ecstatic gift of tongues. After all, in the Corinthian way of thinking (and, sadly, in the thinking of many Christians today), if one had an ecstatic gift, it granted that person a superior status because of the "special revelation" received. This group, or at least this mind-set, is still alive today under many names, always seeking a deeper, hidden truth. Paul used the word *mystery* to set it in contrast with the dark mysteries of pagan religion. Unlike the pagan mysteries, which are kept hidden and revealed only as one makes progress through the ranks, God reveals His mysteries to everyone who believes.

Look at how Paul used this word to draw the attention of the first-century church. In 1 Corinthians 4:1 pastors are called "stewards of the mysteries of God." In Colossians 4:3–4 Paul asked for prayer so that "God would open…a door of utterance, to speak the mystery of Christ…that I may make it [the mystery] manifest" (KJV). In Ephesians 1:9 Paul says that God has "made known to us the mystery of His will, according to His good pleasure which He purposed in Himself." Also, in a clear co-opting of the pagan religion's language, Paul in Colossians 2:2–3 expresses his hope that their "hearts may be encouraged, being knit together in love, and attaining to all riches of the full assurance of understanding, to the knowledge of the mystery of God, both of the Father and of Christ, *in whom are hidden all the treasures of wisdom and knowledge*" (emphasis added).

In stark contrast to voodoo, special knowledge, secret rites, Masonic teaching, Scientology, et al., our message, the mystery of Christ, and the mysteries of God are not just to be protected but also boldly proclaimed. Being able to present these mysteries is a glorious privilege. The Word of God takes us into the prehistoric times in the counsels of eternity. Back in Ephesians 1 we see that the mystery of God is directly related to our salvation. Paul said that "in Him [Christ] also we have obtained an inheritance, being predestined according to the purpose of Him who works all things according to the counsel of His will, that we who first trusted in Christ should be to the praise of His glory" (vv. 11–12).

But the "miracle of Christ in me is the mystery that sets me free." What is that mystery, and why is it so important?

THE MIRACLE OF CHRIST

Back in 1 Timothy 3:16 we find an ancient hymn of praise. That passage declares that the great mystery has been revealed in the appearing of God in the human flesh of Jesus. We have discussed in other chapters how Jesus did not meet the expectations of not only the religious leaders of His day but also of the general idea of the Messiah. Few were expecting the Lord to come the way He came. The Jews were, for the most part, looking for an earthly king. The Greco-Roman world was expecting the intervention of Zeus in mighty power.

The coming of Christ surprised the world. Being born of a virgin in a stable in a little village called Bethlehem of humble parents (and questionable parentage) was not what was expected. Jews were looking to Jerusalem among the mighty, while Romans had declared Caesar to be their god.

But the person of God could be seen on the face of a baby cradled in Bethlehem. In the flesh of Jesus of Nazareth the God of all the ages flashed forth His deity. From the cradle to the cross Jesus surprised those who met Him. Though He adhered to the religion of His people, He was not religious but spiritual. Though He had the authority to call down legions of angels and even, indeed, to wipe out humanity from existence and to start the entire process over, He was gentle. He was firm and loving. He was human and divine. He was life, but He was put to death on a cross for our sins. He is the God-man.

A god dying was not unheard of in the mythologies of the ancient world, but God dying for the purpose of the salvation of His creation was unheard of. What a wonderful surprise for the world to learn the long-hidden mystery: God loves and cares for *and suffers* for His people. The late C. S. Lewis wrote many wonderful books in defense of Christianity. He had been an unbeliever who had ridiculed Christ for many years. He was converted and wrote a book about his conversion entitled *Surprised by Joy*. It's true; it is still a wonderful surprise to discover Jesus.

But the mystery is also a supernatural one. There are those who would deny the supernatural truth of our faith, but Christ, His life, and His ministry were surrounded by the supernatural. The Holy Spirit was prominent in the earthly life of Jesus from even before Jesus was born. At Jesus's conception the Holy Spirit settled into the womb of Mary and supernaturally impregnated that little virgin, conceiving in her womb the only begotten Son of God who was, therefore, fully human but also fully God.

The Holy Spirit

The Holy Spirit descended upon Jesus at His baptism, and Scripture declares that Jesus was full of the Spirit. I also believe that the Holy Spirit was at work in the life of Jesus before that. We see that at the age of twelve, before He would have been considered a "man" by His culture, Jesus sat in the temple and taught the Pharisees. In response to His mother's admonitions, He declared, "Did you not know that I must be about My Father's business?" (Luke 2:49). But that moment of Holy Spirit baptism at the public water baptism of Jesus was the empowerment by the Holy Spirit to do the ministry God had called Jesus to do as a Spirit-filled man. He announced the beginning of His ministry by quoting Isaiah 61:1: "The Spirit of the Lord GOD is upon Me."

Angels

Additionally the miracle of Jesus was attested to by angels. With trumpet voice they heralded His birth over the shepherd's field in Bethlehem. At His temptation Jesus entered into warfare with Satan, and when the skirmish was over, the angels came to minister to Jesus. In Gethsemane when the disciples slept and the stress of the imminent ordeal began to overwhelm Jesus's body so much so that His capillaries broke and He began to sweat blood, the angels came and ministered strength to Him. There atop Calvary seventy-two thousand angels stood with drawn swords, ready to rescue Him who was heaven's delight, but He did not call them. The empty tomb was presided over by angels who first declared, "He is not here. He is risen!" (Matt. 28:6). At His ascension angels said, "Why do you stand gazing up into heaven? This same Jesus, who was taken up from you into heaven, will so come in like manner as you saw Him go into heaven" (Acts 1:11). His angels watched over Him.

Salvation

Before His ascension Jesus gave the Great Commission, charging that the gospel was to be preached to all nations and that His followers were to make disciples of all people. We are to declare this revelation of Christ, this divine mystery, to our world. Both the method of declaring the message and the requirements still surprise the world. The message is to be preached, and the requirement to be saved is belief.

When we witness today that some are still surprised to learn that a person is saved by faith, what we have to realize is that the mystery of Christ is still to so many people just that: a mystery. They cannot (or they refuse to) comprehend that salvation could come outside of our own good works. "But I'm a good person," they say. "I go to church." "I recycle." "I give food to homeless people." "I drive an electric car." (I'm not even kidding about that last one.) They say these things in defense of their goodness and in support of the reasons that they are both "good" and heaven bound.

Salvation comes when we believe in Christ enough to commit our lives to Him for time and eternity. It is not our works, our perceived goodness, our family lineage, or anything else that saves us. It is only the miracle of "Christ in you" (Col. 1:27) that saves you.

The Mystery Revealed

Many years ago there was a television program called *I've Got a Secret*. In this program a guest would whisper a secret to the host, who would then give a panel the opportunity to guess the secret. God is not playing *I've Got a Secret* with us. Every time the word *mystery* is used in the New Testament, it always refers to God revealing a truth. God's mysteries are open secrets. That said, the miracle of Christ in you is this: "The Spirit of Him who raised Jesus from the dead dwells in you!" (Rom. 8:11). Yes, if you are a Christian, then the same Spirit that raised Christ from the dead is alive and in you right now! Let's look at what that means.

Since God gave the Holy Spirit to enable Jesus to do the work God called Him to do, God will also give the Holy Spirit to enable you to do the work God has called you to do. Since God released angels to minister to Jesus through some of His most trying times, God will release angels to minister to you during your times of trial, pain, and suffering. Since God has released salvation through the shed blood of Jesus, you can freely partake of that salvation without worrying that your works are not good enough to get the job of your salvation done.

Years ago a missionary named David Morse was trying to share the gospel with a native of India named Rambhau. The poor man simply could not see how God could save him without works. Rambhau told Morse he would crawl on his knees to Delhi to prove his love for God. Though the islander disagreed with the missionary, he loved him and offered the proselytizer his most precious possession: a large pearl that had been recovered by the man's own son. The Indian explained that his son had drowned while diving for pearls, and this rare gem had been clenched in the young boy's hand when the body was retrieved from the water.

David Morse said, "I cannot take it, but I will buy it from you."

"I want to give it to you," the old man replied. "My son died for it. It is priceless."

The missionary answered, "Can't you see that you have insulted God by trying to work for or earn salvation? His Son, Jesus, died that He might give you the most priceless gift!"[1]

Do not be surprised at the mystery that God has given His Son to save you. Yes, the miracle of "Christ in you" is indeed the mystery that sets you and me free.

Chapter 13

The MYSTERY *of the* MAGI

A MONG THE MANY glories of Christmas are the mysterious strangers called the wise men. There is much mystery surrounding them, but we have been anesthetized and, in many ways, brainwashed about these pilgrims who journeyed from the east in search of the newborn King. I know that sounds harsh, but ask yourself this: How many wise men were present at the birth of Jesus? Three, right? That one should be easy. There are, after all, three wise men in virtually every nativity scene, display, or pageant at Christmastime, be that display on a fireplace mantle, the verdant lawn of a home, or the aisles of your church sanctuary.

However, the true answer to that question is none. I'll get to why in a moment, but we do not even know how many wise men there were in total. We do, however, know that they were not there at the birth of Jesus. They were not there at the stable in Bethlehem.

But who were they? The word in the New Testament is *magos*, which technically means a "Magian" (a scientist from the Orient) but usually implied a magician. This is, in fact, where we get our word *magician*. But these men, the text clearly shows, were ancient interpreters of the stars who combined primitive astronomy with astrology.

We are almost certain that they came from the Medes, which is modern-day Iran. In the history of the Medes this term *magos* came to mean "commander." Under the rule of Cyrus we find magi first mentioned as priest-commanders. They were more than likely adherents or priests of the religion of Zoroastrianism.

The interesting thing here is that the magi regarded the Book of Daniel as holy and were very familiar with its prophecies. Having looked at this background, we need to ask some serious questions, specifically: What was that Star of Bethlehem? Were the Magi just lucky? Most severely, were these star watchers part of some occultic practice?

THE STAR

It sounds good in the story and works really well in song, but when you really think about "the star of Bethlehem," it is weird on a lot of levels. Scientifically it would be easy to dismiss the appearance of the light of a star in the night sky as portentous, because any appearance would have been caused by an event long before it would have been visible to us. Supernaturally, however, we affirm that God can do anything. But, all of that aside, there are the greater questions: Why a star? Is that even biblical? Does the Old Testament mention a star in any kind of messianic prophecy or in relation to the birth of Jesus?

The answer is yes! Look at Numbers 24:17:

> I see Him, but not now; I behold Him, but not near; a Star shall come out of Jacob; a Scepter shall rise out of Israel, and batter the brow of Moab, and destroy all the sons of tumult.

There is a strong Jewish tradition that a star would appear when the long-expected Messiah should come. In fact, within about a century of Jesus's ministry, death, and resurrection, there arose a man named Simon bar Kokhba, who led what was called the Bar Kokhba revolt. Right up until the moment he died, he was believed by many to be the Messiah. His popular name, which was lent to the name of the revolt, means "son of a star."

But this sounds a bit like star worship or astrology. Does the Bible give any credence to messages from the stars? The answer, though a surprising one to many I am sure, is a resounding yes!

Both Old and New Testaments clearly speak of the witness of God's vast creation. Notice the first clear mention of a star in the Bible in Genesis 1:14–15:

> Then God said, "Let there be lights in the firmament of the heavens to divide the day from the night; and *let them be for signs and seasons*, and for days and years; and let them be for lights in the firmament of the heavens to give light on the earth"; and it was so.
>
> —EMPHASIS ADDED

The stars are signs! They are not simply massive, luminous spheres of plasma held together by gravity. They are specific points in the second heaven, placed with intent by the Creator of everything! In Psalm 147:4 we read that God "counts the number of the stars [and] He calls them all by name."

Zodiac

Before I proceed, I must take a moment to preemptively defend myself against those who would say or even think that I am endorsing astrology or the reading or use of horoscopes. This is simply not true. I stand by what the Bible teaches about these things. For example, in Deuteronomy 18:10–11:

> There shall not be found among you anyone who makes his son or his daughter pass through the fire, or one who practices witchcraft, or a soothsayer, or one who interprets omens, or a sorcerer, or one who conjures spells, or a medium, or a spiritist, or one who calls up the dead.

And later in Isaiah 47:13–14:

> You are wearied in the multitude of your counsels; let now the astrologers, the stargazers, and the monthly prognosticators stand up and save you from what shall come upon you. Behold, they shall be as stubble, the fire shall burn them; they

shall not deliver themselves from the power of the flame; it shall not be a coal to be warmed by, nor a fire to sit before!

Yet the names of the constellations predate occultic astrology. In fact, the names of these are found in Scripture. In the Book of Job and in the Book of Amos the constellations of Pleiades and Orion are mentioned. In the Hebrew Bible are found references to Ursa Major and the entirety of the Mazzaroth. The word *mazzaroth* was created to describe what we know as the circle of the Zodiac, but its original meaning is "way." The names of these stars and constellations date back as far as 5000 BC, and Flavius Josephus, Ptolemy, and other ancient historians and astronomers support their use as a circular story.

THE STARS AND THE GOSPEL

Psalm 19:1 is often used as an opening foundation verse for creationists, and that is, I think, a perfectly valid use for it. However, when the first section of the psalm is read in its entirety, a fascinating declaration is revealed:

> The heavens declare the glory of God; and the firmament shows His handiwork. Day unto day utters speech, and night unto night reveals knowledge. There is no speech nor language where their voice is not heard. Their line has gone out through all the earth, and their words to the end of the world. In them He has set a tabernacle for the sun, which is like a bridegroom coming out of his chamber, and rejoices like a strong man to run its race. Its rising is from one end of heaven, and its circuit to the other end; and there is nothing hidden from its heat.
> —PSALM 19:1–6

What an astounding passage. David says that there is, in the very fabric of creation, a story declaring God's work. Even in the context of Paul's evangelism this truth is declared. Remember his words found in Romans 10:17. Paul wrote, "So then faith comes by hearing, and hearing by the word of God." Remember that this statement is not simply about evangelizing those who have not heard the gospel. Paul is speaking very specifically about Israel and her relationship to messianic prophecy and truth. Paul asks back in verse 14:

> How then shall they call on Him in whom they have not believed? And how shall they believe in Him of whom they have not heard? And how shall they hear without a preacher?

But then Paul asks an interesting rhetorical question in verse 18:

> But I say, have they not heard? Yes indeed: "Their sound has gone out to all the earth, and their words to the ends of the world."

Paul says that Israel, and, by extension, everyone, is without excuse because the truth of God is written in the stars.

I will not go too in-depth with this, but there have been fascinating studies made of the story that the constellations tell. You can see a list of these books in the bibliography, but the short version is this: if you start with the constellation Virgo and cycle through to the constellation Leo, there is a complete ancient prophecy of the coming of Messiah and the life of Jesus.

THE STAR OF BETHLEHEM

So it is plain that God has used the stars as signs for eons, but in this chapter we are focusing on one star—and the men who followed it—in particular. It is very difficult to know with certainty what the true nature of this phenomenon was, but there are some interesting theories.

Some scholars think it might have been a comet, as the comet was, traditionally, a celestial object connected with important events such as the birth of a king. The early church father Origen proposed that it might have been a *sui-hsing*, or "broom star." However, neither this nor other records of comet sightings match up with the time that Jesus was born.

There is also the possibility that it was not a star specifically but a conjunction, or gathering, of planets in the night sky. The problem is that as bright as a conjunction can appear, especially in a pre-technological world, any conjunction would not have lasted the amount of time necessary for the record of Scripture to be accurate.

Some postulate that an exploding star, or supernova, was the actual Christmas star. A supernova can produce an extraordinary amount of light comparably, but again, historical records do not indicate a supernova at the time of the Lord's birth.

Still others believe that the celestial light was no star at all but was, in fact, a supernatural light visible only to the wise men. I dismiss this theory, because when the magi spoke with King Herod and said, "We have seen His star in the East" (Matt. 2:2), neither Herod nor his priests and scribes dismissed the star's existence.

So what was it?

I am convinced that the star of Bethlehem was a real star that showed up in the constellation Virgo prior to the birth of Jesus and continued to shine for about seven years. The apocryphal Gospel of James, written by the brother of Jesus, and writings of the first-century bishop Ignatius describe the star as dazzling, with Ignatius saying that it "outshone all the celestial lights, and to which the Sun and Moon did obeisance."[1]

FOLLOWING THE LIGHT

It is amazing to me that these wise men—Gentiles, pagans—were the only people able to discern the signs of their time from the pages of Jewish Scripture. They had limited scriptural knowledge. Yet while they were in darkness, the little light they had led them on a journey to discover God made flesh, the little babe in the manger, the precious child named Jesus.

So often I hear people say that it would be easier for them to believe in God if only God would give them a sign. Then I think about these magi. They had one sign, one tiny ray of light, one small passage of, for them, a foreign text of a foreign people who worshipped a foreign God: a four-hundred-year-old promise from Daniel:

> Seventy weeks are determined for your people and for your holy city, to finish the transgression, to make an end of sins, to make reconciliation for iniquity, to bring in everlasting righteousness, to seal up vision and prophecy, and to anoint the Most Holy.
>
> Know therefore and understand, that from the going forth of the command to restore and build Jerusalem until Messiah the Prince, there shall be seven weeks and sixty-two weeks; the street shall be built again, and the wall, even in troublesome times.
>
> And after the sixty-two weeks Messiah shall be cut off, but not for Himself; and the people of the prince who is to come shall destroy the city and the sanctuary. The end of it shall be with a flood, and till the end of the war desolations are determined.
>
> —Daniel 9:24–26

You see, Daniel would have been important to these men. Recall that Daniel was made ruler of the entire province of Babylon, and he was chief administrator over all the wise men of Babylon. He, Daniel, was in many ways one of their practical ancestors.

In addition to this prophecy that pointed out a specific time period in which Messiah, "the Prince" or ruler, would appear, another interesting point to note here is that when the magi appeared before Herod, they made an interesting claim:

> Where is He who has been born King of the Jews? For we have
> seen His star in the East and have come to worship Him.
> —MATTHEW 2:2

There seemed to be no doubt in their mind that the star that appeared in Virgo was "His" star—that it was a special celestial event that proclaimed the birth of the King.

WISE ROLE MODELS

There are some important things to note about these sojourners who came to find a king. First, look at how they are described. In Matthew 2:1 it says that they were wise men "from the East." This phrase comes from the Greek word *anatole*. This beautiful word means "rising of the sun." They came from the sunrise. Their visit marked the beginning of a new day.

Second, they had a spirit of faith. Now, we have already mentioned that Paul established the fact that faith comes by hearing, and hearing by the Word of God. The Bible makes it clear that faith is a gift of God, and these men had it in spades. Their faith made them unafraid to set out on a journey to a faraway land; a journey that involved their leaving hearth and home; a journey on which they carried priceless treasures and risked not only their lives but also the lives of those in their caravan.

Third, note how these men were willing to be moved out of their comfort zone. It cannot be stressed enough that these men were practitioners of a wholly different religion. They had cultural, religious, and familial differences from the people they were going to see. They left the land of their king (probably Arsaces XXV) to find another king. How willing would you be to go search out a king based on a short passage written four hundred years earlier?

Additionally I find it amazing that these men were not at all afraid to ask questions. Remember that when they reached Jerusalem, they obtained an audience with Herod (not an easy feat, and this fact speaks to their prominence and wealth). They had gone as far as they could go based on the evidence they had, and now they needed more information. They were seekers! They were inquisitive!

Before I move away form this point, I would like to make one more observation. These wise men approached the man called "king" in order to find the King for whom they had traveled so far. We know the aftermath of this encounter, but I find it merciful that God gave Herod a chance to do the right thing. But instead of availing himself of God's mercy, Herod attempted to use the wise men to discover the supposed usurper's identity and kill Him. How sad it is when God lays a revelation in our laps and we refuse to see it.

When Herod could give them no assistance, the wise men demonstrated that they were willing to be led by God. Read Matthew 2:9:

> When they heard the king, they departed; and behold, the star which they had seen in the East went before them, till it came and stood over where the young Child was.

I concede that at this point, the star could have been miraculous and not merely a physical phenomenon. The point, however, is that these men showed incredible faith in following a star to find the answer to their questions.

Finally these men were not afraid to express joy. Read Matthew's description of that first encounter:

> When they saw the star, they rejoiced with exceedingly great joy. And when they had come into the house, they saw the young Child with Mary His mother, and fell down and worshiped Him. And when they had opened their treasures, they presented gifts to Him: gold, frankincense, and myrrh.
>
> —Matthew 2:10–11

BOWING IN WORSHIP

The imagery and even the words here are important enough to dwell on for a while.

Take note of a few important phrases. First, "They rejoiced with exceedingly great joy." In the simplest way that I can describe it, the Bible says that these men acted after the manner of the most rabid football fan on Super Bowl Sunday when his team wins. They danced and sang "vehemently" at their discovery. That's what the word *exceedingly* means.

These men were shouting, shaking, singing—and it was a flooding overflow that could not be contained. Not only was their joy "exceeding," but it was also "great." What does that mean? The word in Greek is *megas*. They did not have normal, everyday joy. These wise men, at the discovery of Jesus, had *mega* joy!

Next, take note that they "fell down and worshiped Him." First, let that image sink in. They had traveled thousands of miles, and now they had finally found the object of their search. There, in a tiny home, bouncing on the knee of a virginal mother, was a one-year-old baby boy. And they fell down before Him and worshipped!

Now for all of my straitlaced, no-nonsense brothers and sisters in Christ who think that some of the stuff that we do at Abba's House is silly and unbiblical because "Why would God ever want anybody to just fall down during a service?", I want you to take note: this phrase indicates that when they fell, it was a completely involuntary fall.

This same word, in the same sense, is used in the following passages:

> Therefore whoever hears these sayings of Mine, and does them, I will liken him to a wise man who built his house on the rock: and the rain descended, the floods came, and the winds blew and beat on that house; and it did not fall, for it was founded on the rock.
>
> But everyone who hears these sayings of Mine, and does

not do them, will be like a foolish man who built his house on the sand: and the rain descended, the floods came, and the winds blew and beat on that house; and it fell. And great was its fall.

—MATTHEW 7:24–27

And:

But in those days, after that tribulation, the sun will be darkened, and the moon will not give its light; the stars of heaven will fall, and the powers in the heavens will be shaken.

—MARK 13:24–25

And:

Or those eighteen on whom the tower in Siloam fell and killed them, do you think that they were worse sinners than all other men who dwelt in Jerusalem?

—LUKE 13:4

There are so many others places this word used. The word in Greek is *piptō* or *petō*. It means an involuntary fall; a fall that cannot be helped. So were these men "slain in the Spirit"? It seems as if they were. They had found the King. What an awesome sight to see these mighty, powerful men humble themselves in worship before the infant King Jesus!

Finally, look at how they worshipped. The word used here is one we have mentioned in other places. *Proskuneō* means to "kiss toward" or "first kiss." It was often used of lovers but was also used to denote a pet licking the feet and hand of its master. Here were these great men bowing down to kiss the feet of a toddling boy. How astounding!

Also, these men, the Bible says, "opened their treasures" (Matt. 2:11) The word *treasure* comes from the Greek word *thesaurus*. It means "wealth." I won't get too technical here, but all of the verbs and participles in this passage are in the aorist tense. What that means is that the opening of these treasures was for the magi an effective, successful, single, one-time action. However, though it was a one-time event, the effect of it lasted throughout the life of Jesus (and possibly further).

The gifts speak to the very nature, life, and purpose of Jesus. The magi gave gold, which pointed to the fact that Jesus was a king. The frankincense they gave was used in temple rites, and the aroma of it is said to represent life. Therefore, the frankincense represented Jesus's presence. Finally, the myrrh they gave pointed toward Jesus's crucifixion and eventual death. Myrrh was used to anoint dead bodies for burial.

THE MYSTERY REVEALED

There is so much to unpack from the lives of these men. It amazes me still that these men, whose appearance takes up barely half of one short chapter in one Gospel, have so much to teach us about the Christian life.

First of all, there is the understanding that God speaks to us through His creation. I know that this is mentioned in Psalm 19, but to know that the God who created everything took time to place lights in the sky that would for thousands of years testify to not only what He was going to do but also what He has done is an amazing thing. Why would He, for lack of a better way to put it, take the time to do that? He must care so much about you and me!

Also, I am humbled by the faith of these magi. But I am more humbled that the faith God placed in them is nothing compared to what He is willing to place in me! I think back to these men, and I see that their story demonstrates that because of Jesus's birth, there is hope for a new day—that I too can have a hunger for a living God, a heart for faith's adventure, but most importantly that I can have humility to embrace the change that Jesus wants to work in my life.

Of highest importance though is that the life of these men

speaks not only to how I should but how I *get* to worship my King. Real worship holds nothing back. The magi gave extravagantly. So should we! Their worship was guided by faith in God's Word. So should ours be! Their worship was persistent. So should we be! Their worship was joyful, and they would not settle for less than seeing and knowing Jesus. We should settle for nothing less! Yes, the real mystery of the wise men, these magi, these priest-commanders, is that their lives, those of pagans who knew nothing of Christ except that He was a promised king, show us that God truly is not willing that any should perish and that He will reveal Himself to any, even those outside of the promise, who will diligently seek Him.

Chapter 14

The MYSTERY *of the* EMPTY TOMB

I
F THERE IS a stony place that cries out louder than any other on the face of the earth, it is that little place right outside the Damascus Gate, just beyond a skull-shaped cliff called Calvary. Just a stone's throw away from that cliff is the empty tomb. It is, without exaggeration, the hinge of history. There are two sites that claim to be the actual burial place of Jesus. One is the Church of the Holy Sepulcher, and the other is the Garden Tomb. I am firmly convinced that the Garden Tomb is the authentic site.

The location of Jesus's tomb was well known to the post-apostolic church. In AD 333 a pilgrim from Bordeaux, France, wrote, "As you pass through the gate of Neapolis (Damscus Gate)...on your left in the hillock, [is] Golgotha where the Lord was crucified, and about a stone's throw from it, [is] the vault where they lay His body and He rose again on the third day."[1] This is the exact location of the Garden Tomb and what is known as Gordon's Calvary. We know from Scripture that the cross and the tomb were near each other. John 19:42 tells us, "So there they laid Jesus, because of the Jews' Preparation Day, for the tomb was nearby."

Calvary is located on Mount Moriah where the mountain has been quarried in half. Oddly the jagged cliff, situated near Jeremiah's grotto, looks like a skull. Muslims had turned this area into a garbage dump, but in the late nineteenth century, Major General Charles George Gordon excavated this area and found what has now come to be called the Garden Tomb.[2] It has some peculiar evidences:

- No human bones were found in the area.

- There is a slot for a stone to roll.

- There is an "anchor cross" on the outside wall.

- There are carvings of the Greek letters alpha and omega.

- It is in close proximity to Skull Hill (Calvary).

Now let's move to the narrative of Jesus's life and death and explore the mystery of the tomb.

WAS THE TOMB REALLY EMPTY?

The amazing thing is that the birth, life, ministry, death, and even the resurrection of Jesus are prophesied in Scripture. In Psalm 16:10 we read:

> For You will not leave my soul in Sheol, nor will You allow Your Holy One to see corruption.

The very nature of the resurrection is attested to.

The great evidence for the resurrection of Jesus Christ is the evidence of the narratives themselves. These stand up to the most stringent of critical scrutiny. To begin with, there are four independent accounts. These were not made up in collusion, for if they had been, they would not possess the number of apparent contradictions they contain, such as the number of angels at the tomb, the number of women who went to the garden, the time of their arrival, and other points. These accounts can be harmonized, but the point is that those apparent discrepancies would have been eliminated if the writers had colluded to invent a story. On the other hand, it is also apparent that they did not make up the stories separately because, if they had done that, there would never have been the large measure of overriding agreement they possess. Thus, the setting and the characters are the same, the sequence of events makes sense, and so on. Therefore, if the accounts were not made up in collusion, and if they were not made up separately, the only remaining possibility is that they were not made up at all. They are, simply, four true and independent accounts by those who knew what they were writing.

The broken seal

It is hard for us to not relegate some of these facts to "movie truth." That is, some of the aspects of the narrative have the air of the disclaimers at the beginning of some so-called historical drama films. You know the kind. They say things such as:

> This story is based on actual events. In certain cases incidents, characters, and timelines have been changed for dramatic purposes. Certain characters may be composites or entirely fictitious.

The Roman seal that secured the tomb has been the object of scrutiny for some time. But what we must remember is that this Jesus was a wildly controversial character, and rumors of His claim of resurrection were circulating before He was even arrested. So it comes as no surprise, then, that we read in Matthew 27:62–66:

> On the next day, which followed the Day of Preparation, the chief priests and Pharisees gathered together to Pilate, saying, "Sir, we remember, while He was still alive, how that deceiver said, 'After three days I will rise.' Therefore command that the tomb be made secure until the third day, lest His disciples come by night and steal Him away, and say to the people, 'He has risen from the dead.' So the last deception will be worse than the first."
> Pilate said to them, "You have a guard; go your way, make it as secure as you know how." So they went and made the tomb secure, sealing the stone and setting the guard.

Now picture the scene. There are guards standing before the tomb, and the stone has been sealed. According to the historian Justin in his Treatise 49, the breaking of a Roman seal was a capital offense. Does it seem rational that the tomb would have been guarded and sealed in an effort to preemptively disprove any story of Jesus's resurrection without those in power having ensured that the body was in the tomb? Moreover, which of the cowardly disciples do you think would even have approached that tomb with the guard present, and the risk of death, for fear of being charged with tampering with the Roman seal? Bearing in mind these facts, it is certain that Jesus's body was secured in the tomb before the seal was placed on the covering stone.

The great stone

Yet the stone was rolled away. In Mark 16 we read that the women, Mary Magdalene, Mary the mother of James, and Salome, were bringing spices that they might come and anoint the body of Jesus. They said to themselves, "Who will roll away the stone from the door of the tomb for us?" (v. 3) It is evident here that the women were unaware of the placing of the seal and the men guarding it. But in verse 4 of that same chapter we read these wonderful words: "But when they looked up, they saw that the stone had been rolled away—for it was very large."

Yes, the stone was large. If we use the Garden Tomb as the template, we have to consider the size of the entrance. The opening is big enough to enter without bending, and would have taken a stone of five and a half to six feet in diameter to cover it. The groove in front of the opening, which was cut into the rock, has a deep indentation at the entrance and is about one foot thick. A stone of the size that would fit in this spot would have weighed one and a half to two tons and would have taken several very strong men a considerable amount of time to dislodge it.

The state of the tomb

Consider, as well, the absence of the *corpus dilecti* (proof of a crime) and that the clothes found were undisturbed. (See the chapter in this book on the Shroud of Turin.)

The change in the disciples

In the closing chapters of the Gospels, we see a group of men as cowardly as any who have ever walked the earth. They are defeated. They are downtrodden. Peter—who in the Garden of Gethsemane had drawn his sword and cut off the ear of one of the high priest's servants and then run like a coward (to the point of swearing at a little servant girl and denying that he, Peter, had ever even heard of Jesus) when Jesus rebuked him—had decided to just go back to being a fisherman. But in fifty short days these men went from being cowards running scared to being emboldened proclaimers who had witnessed with their own eyes the risen Christ. So profound was their change, so profound was the truth they unleashed on the world, that they were willing to die for it.

THE CONVERSION OF JAMES

I will linger on this one, because this evidence, for me, bears more weight than anything else one might read of the first-century church. Mary, the mother of Jesus, had other children. We are not certain exactly how many, but the Gospels clearly state that Jesus had brothers. The most noted of these is James, who would become the head of the church at Jerusalem.

Read the striking introductory wording of the letter of James in the New Testament:

> James, a bondservant of God and of the Lord Jesus Christ, to the twelve tribes which are scattered abroad: Greetings.

The verbiage here is pretty, but it loses something, I think, in our colloquial understanding. James did not declare himself to be a "bondservant" as we understand it. He proclaimed himself to be a "slave" to God and of the Lord Jesus Christ.

It is so striking to me that James never seemed to play on his genealogy. So often in the church we see people climbing up the coattails of their familial standing in a local body. Worse still are the ones who assume salvation just because their grandmas went to church every time the doors were open and, often, brought them to church. Let me tell you, friend, God does not have grandchildren!

James does not do any of that. In the human sense it would seem simple and even prudent that he would address his letter by reminding his intended readers that he was Jesus's brother. But he does not do that. In 1 Corinthians 15:6–7 we find the only real deference to James, where we read:

> After that [Jesus] was seen by over five hundred brethren at once, of whom the greater part remain to the present, but some have fallen asleep. After that He was seen by James, then by all the apostles.

This is the only place where James is really singled out, and it is in a context of Paul defending the truth of the empty tomb.

Another poignant note is that James was often referred to as "camel knees," because his fervent dedication to prayer caused calluses to develop on his knees. And it was this James who, through the leading of the Holy Spirit, brought the famous phrase "the effective, fervent prayer of a righteous man avails much" (James 5:16) to the world. James was greatly changed by the empty tomb.

THE MYSTERY REVEALED

All of these are important, but whether the empty tomb is to be found at the Church of the Holy Sepulcher or the empty tomb is to be found at the Garden Tomb, the most important thing we can take away from it is this: the tomb is empty!

Famed British educator and historian Thomas Arnold said

that the resurrection of Jesus Christ is the best attested fact in history.[3] Writing under the name Frank Morison, Albert Henry Ross set out to disprove the resurrection of Christ. In the end this brilliant lawyer was converted and wrote the classic book *Who Moved the Stone?*[4] In a letter to the Rev. E. L. Macassey, the distinguished British jurist Sir Edward Clark wrote:

> As a lawyer I have made a prolonged study of the evidences for the events of the first Easter Day. To me the evidence is conclusive, and over and over again in the High Court I have secured the verdict on evidence not nearly so compelling. Inference follows on evidence, and a truthful witness is always artless and disdains effect. The Gospel evidence for the resurrection is of this class, and as a lawyer I accept it unreservedly as the testimony of men to facts that were able to substantiate it.[4]

Lea Wallace sought to disprove Christ's resurrection and was so soundly converted that it moved him to write his magnificent novel *Ben-Hur*. In the drama *The Trial of Jesus* John Masefield pictures Longinus, a Roman centurion, talking with the wife of Pontius Pilate about the details of Jesus' death. She questions him, "Do you believe He is dead? The centurion replies, "No, lady, I don't." Pilate's wife probes, "Then where is He?" And the soldier answers, "Let loose on the world, lady, where no man, neither Roman nor Jew, can stop His truth."[6] John Warwick Montgomery of the Dean Simon Greenleaf School of Law said:

> It passes the bonds of credibility that the early Christians could have manufactured such a tale and then preached it among those who might easily have refuted it *simply by producing the body.*[7]
>
> —EMPHASIS ADDED

Anyone who neglects the fact of the resurrection has not begun to deal with life.

Dr. R. W. White, one of God's great Christian statesmen, told of a brilliant Chinese man who came to services that White was conducting. The young man asked for a New Testament and was given one. Later he came to confess Christ and gave this stirring testimony:

> I took the New Testament home with me. I sat down on the floor and read it through before I did anything else. I have read the great writings of Confucius. I wanted to satisfy my hungry heart there. I knocked at the door but no answer came for Confucius was dead. I read the message of Buddhism seeking that for which my soul so profoundly longed. I knocked at the door of Buddha but no answer came for Buddha was dead. I read the Koran. My soul longed to find peace there. I knocked at the door but no answer came for Muhammad was dead. I read the writings of the greatest patriots and religious leaders of the past. I knocked but no answer came. While reading this New Testament, I found that it claimed its Author to be alive. I knocked at that door. I found the living Christ. He came into my soul. Here my hungry heart found peace, a peace for which it has longed.[8]

Perhaps you were raised in church or you never joined a church; maybe doubt has been sown into you; maybe you never really believed that Jesus is alive. I pray that you understand that I'm not talking about a myth or a fable. The answer, friend, the mystery revealed, is that Jesus Christ is Lord, and the empty tomb proves it! The same Jesus who came out of that grave has made it possible for the same "Spirit of Him who raised Jesus from the dead dwells in you, [and] He who raised Christ from the dead will also give life to your mortal bodies through His Spirit who dwells in you" (Rom. 8:11).

Chapter 15

The MYSTERY *of the* SHROUD *of* TURIN

IN TURIN, ITALY, in a small chapel behind the altar in the Cathedral of Saint John the Baptist, is stored an ancient burial cloth. The cloth is fourteen feet, three inches by three feet, seven inches. On the cloth is an amber color in the image of an adult man who has been crucified. There are marks on the figure as if from the Roman whip, nail marks on the wrists and ankles. There also appear to be wounds around its forehead consistent with a crown of thorns having been pressed there.[1]

There are people who say that the shroud is a clever work of art. Others say it is the genuine burial cloth of Jesus Christ. For the longest time the primary argument against the shroud's veracity was a carbon 14 dating test. In 1988 the carbon 14 test was done, showing the shroud to be a fourteenth-century item.[2] The history of the shroud proved it to be older than that. It was found that the fibers tested were from a three-inch space near an area damaged by a fire in 1532.[3]

A BRIEF HISTORY

The shroud surfaced right around the time of the crucifixion, death, and resurrection of Jesus. The Syriac king Abgar V the Black (or Abgarus V of Edessa) was, according to tradition, one of the first Christian kings in history, having been converted by the evangelism of the apostle Thaddeus of Edessa (thought to be one of the seventy-two disciples sent by Jesus in Luke 10:1). He is said to have been healed when he viewed an image of Christ brought on a cloth from Jerusalem. Around AD 57 his son became ruler of Edessa (a city located near the southeast border of Turkey today known as Urfa), and it was at this point that the shroud vanished from history for almost five centuries.

Around 944 the conquering Roman army demanded the cloth possibly as the price of peace. It was then moved from Edessa, Turkey, to Constantinople (Istanbul). There is historical evidence that the cloth was on display in Constantinople in the early years of the twelfth century.

In early 1204 the shroud was taken from that city, presumably by Crusaders. Tradition says that it fell into the hands of a group of warrior monks called Knights Templar. Ian Wilson reports that there is evidence that Marquis Boniface de Montferrat, who led the attack on the chapel in Constantinople where the shroud was kept, brought the shroud to his friend Otto de la Roche in Athens, Greece. It was he who gave it to the Templar Knights.[4]

In 1307 the Knights Templar were charged with idolatry for worshipping an image on a cloth. They would hold night meetings and adore and kiss the image of Christ. For its protection it is thought the knights carried the shroud to France.[5]

The Knights of Templar were charged with idolatry by the church. Many of them were tried, and some of their leaders were burned at the stake, including Geoffrey de Charny, one of their preceptors. The shroud is believed to have been passed on to a relative, a French knight also named Geoffrey de Charny, who displayed it in 1353. The younger Geoffrey was killed on September 19, 1356. His granddaughter sold the cloth to the Duke of Savoy in 1452.[6] In 1464 the shroud was stored in a chapel in Chambery, France, and was damaged in a fire in 1532.[7] There is a drop of molten silver burned on its edge, and the holes seen in the shroud were punched in 1534.[8] From 1578 till now the shroud has been kept in Turin, Italy.[9]

The other cloth

Not much is heard of the second grave cloth found in Jesus's empty tomb, the one that was wrapped around His head. In John 20:7 we read:

> And the handkerchief that had been around His head, not lying with the linen cloths, [was] folded together in a place by itself.

From 570 onward there are stories and histories of another cloth called the Sudarium of Oviedo. According to Bishop Pelagius this facial cloth was removed from Jerusalem in 614. Studies have shown that an image can be seen with the help of certain lighting and scientific equipment.[10] Here is the mystery! Both the shroud and the Sudarium are stained with type AB blood. When the Sudarium is superimposed on the Shroud of Turin, the facial impressions match.

THE BODY IN THE SHROUD

To understand the circumstances surrounding the Shroud of Turin and its importance, we have to look first to the pages of Scripture. In John 19:39–40 we read:

> And Nicodemus, who at first came to Jesus by night, also came, bringing a mixture of myrrh and aloes, about a hundred pounds. Then they took the body of Jesus, and bound it in strips of linen with the spices, as the custom of the Jews is to bury.

So here we see the first reference to the possibility of a shroud. So what is the possibility that the Shroud of Turin is the same cloth that wrapped the body of Jesus? Dr. Robert J. Bucklin, a forensic pathologist with over fifty years of experience, used state-of-the-art medical technology to perform a medical "autopsy" on the body wrapped in the shroud. His finds are stunning.[11]

Before looking at some of the more salient details, let's start with a general description. According to Bucklin the body in the shroud was an adult male, seventy-one inches from crown to heel, and weighing an estimated one hundred seventy-five pounds. The person was well developed and well nourished. The body appears to have been in a state of rigor, as evidenced by an overall stiffness as well as specific alterations in the appearance of the lower extremities from the posterior aspect. The deceased had long hair, fixed into a ponytail or braid, and a short beard.[12]

Now for the first noteworthy finding. On the front view of the image there is a ring of puncture tracks on the scalp, while the dorsal view shows that the puncture wounds extend around the occipital portion of the scalp in the shape of a wig or crown. Blood has issued from these punctures onto the hair and skin of the forehead, and the direction of the blood flow on front and back is downward. There is a distinct abrasion on the nose, and the right cheek is distinctly swollen when compared to the left cheek.[13]

There is a large bloodstain over the right pectoral region. Close examination shows the presence of two types of fluid, one of blood and the other resembling water. This wound, unlike the others, has distinct characteristics of a postmortem flow of blood from a body cavity or organ. At the uppermost area of the flow is an oval skin defect that is characteristic of a penetrating track made by a sharp puncturing instrument. Additionally there is in increase in the anteroposterior diameter of the chest due to bilateral expansion.[14]

The abdomen is flat, and the arms are crossed over the mid and lower abdomen. Closer inspection of the arms, forearms, wrists, and hands shows the left hand (which is crossed over the right) bears a distinct puncture injury, which has two projecting rivulets. Both flows derive from a central source and are separated by approximately ten degrees. The flows are horizontal in direction and could not have occurred with the arms in the post-mortem position. Calculations indicate that the arms would have to have been outstretched upward at a sixty- to sixty-five-degree angle with the horizontal. The blood flow moves from the wrists inward toward the elbows on both right and left forearms. Inspection of the fingers shows the imprint of only four fingers, with the thumbs not clearly obvious. This suggests that there has been some damage to the nerve, which would result in flexion of the thumb inward toward the palm.[15]

The imprint of the right calf is more distinct than that of the left. This indicates that, upon the time of death, the left leg must have been rotated in such a way that the sole of the left foot was resting on the ventral surface of the right foot. That position was maintained after rigor developed. In the center of the right foot-print, a clear puncture defect is noted. This wound is consistent with an object penetrating the feet, and from the position of the feet the conclusion is that the same object penetrated both feet after the left foot had been placed over the right.[16]

Examination of the dorsal image shows a series of traumatic injuries that extend from the shoulders to the lower back, buttocks, and calves. These images are divided and appear to have been made by an object used in whip-like fashion, leaving dumbbell-shaped imprints in the skin from which blood has issued. The direction of the injuries is lateral to medial and then downward, suggesting that someone to the individual's rear applied the whip. On the shoulder-blades evidence of an abrasion of the skin surfaces is shown. These wounds are consistent with a heavy object such as a beam resting over the shoulder blades and rubbing the skin.[17]

The Ron Phillips translation

I have included a lot of the forensic text partially to let you know that I am not making this up. However, I know it can be confusing, so let me translate the findings.

According to Bucklin there was a man, about seventy-one inches in height and weighing about one hundred seventy-five pounds, who was beaten with fists and/or rods about his face and body, who was also beaten with an open whip from his upper back down to the lower portions of his calves. Some kind of ringlet or crown of a barbed material was put on his head and beaten down into place. A heavy beam was placed on his shoulders, and he was forced to carry this beam while walking.

At some point he was fixed into a position with his hands outstretched at approximately sixty-five degrees, and some kind of object was forced through his hands in such a way that the wound caused severe damage to his median nerve. His legs were brought together, and his feet were placed one on top of the other, and an additional traumatic puncture wound was made, with the singular object penetrating both feet. The man hung suspended for hours, using his feet to raise himself up to gasp giant lungfuls of air and then collapsing due to the pain this caused in his feet.

At some point the man, mercifully, died. After his death a wound was made on the right side of his chest. Some kind of blade penetrated between or under the ribs and caused the fluid that had been collecting in his chest cavity to pour out.

This is what we know for sure about the man wrapped by the Shroud of Turin. But was that man Jesus?

THE BIBLE IN THE SHROUD

Is it possible that the man in the shroud was Jesus? Compare the findings of the forensic pathologist and the biblical accounts.

Beaten

What we know from multiple biblical accounts is that Jesus was beaten. From the time between His arrest in Gethsemane and His final appearance before Pilate, He was beaten with fists and rods of wood. In Mark 14:65 it says:

> Then some began to spit on Him, and to blindfold Him, and to beat Him, and to say to Him, "Prophesy!" And the officers struck Him with the palms of their hands.

And in Luke 23:11 we read:

Then Herod, with his men of war, treated Him with contempt and mocked Him, arrayed Him in a gorgeous robe, and sent Him back to Pilate.

So we see Jesus, even before He was formally accused of anything, being treated with contempt and physical abuse.

Whipped

The nineteenth chapter of John opens with this statement: "So then Pilate took Jesus and scourged Him." In Matthew 27:26 we read, "Then [Pilate] released Barabbas to them; and when he had scourged Jesus, he delivered Him to be crucified." Tradition says that Jesus was whipped thirty-nine times. The film *The Passion of the Christ* shows a brutal beating and flogging that seems to last an intolerable amount of time.

While the Bible does not explicitly say how many lashes Jesus was given, it does say clearly that He was scourged. The word for *scourge* in Greek is *mastigoo*, which, when translated into Latin, is *flagrum*. The device used for this punishment was a standard whip but having two or three to nine (rarely more) thongs. Hard materials such as shards of pottery were affixed to the length of the thongs, and at the end of these tails was a barbell-shaped weight that was often embedded with small hooks. This would cause different kinds of wounds at the same time. The weight of the metal dumbbells would cause deep bruising, while the tiny hooks would rip those places open. The leather of the thongs acted as a belt does, leaving a welt, but the shards of pottery would nick or slice the whipped area.

Scalp wounds

After enduring the beatings, the scourging, and the travesty of a trial, Jesus endured yet more painful humiliation. In Matthew 27 we read that after His scourging, Jesus was brought back, and "the soldiers of the governor took Jesus into the Praetorium and gathered the whole garrison around Him. And they stripped Him and put a scarlet robe on Him. When they had twisted a crown of thorns, they put it on His head, and a reed in His right hand. And they bowed the knee before Him and mocked Him, saying, 'Hail, King of the Jews!' Then they spat on Him, and took the reed and struck Him on the head" (vv. 27–30).

The crown of thorns put on Jesus was not simply placed on His head. The rod that the soldiers had given to Jesus to mock Him as a "king" was taken back from Him, and then it was used to beat the crown of thorns into His brow.

Shoulder wounds

In John 19:17 we read that after enduring the first stages of His torture, Jesus, "bearing His cross, went out to a place called the Place of a Skull, which is called in Hebrew, Golgotha." In virtually every depiction of this scene in the great works of art, Jesus carries His entire cross. This is, more than likely, incorrect. Outside of the fact that the whole cross would have weighed upwards of three hundred fifty pounds (thus rendering it virtually impossible that a person so scourged and beaten would have been physically able to carry the cross in its entirety), history tells a different story. Jesus probably carried just the crossbeam, or the *patibulum*, of His cross. This is still no mean feat. The crossbeam probably weighed between eighty and one hundred fifty pounds.

Additionally the arms of the condemned were tied to the cross in a grim preface of what was to come. This was meant to cause further humiliation and suffering, as the bearer would have no way to catch himself were he to fall. Indeed, tradition says that Jesus fell three times on His way to Calvary (though these accounts are not in Scripture).

Also, give some consideration to the distance Jesus would have traveled with this heavy load. While there is some discrepancy as to where Jesus would have begun the journey, the shortest possible distance He would have traveled is half a mile. I know people who will walk that distance for pleasure and light exercise multiple times a day, so I concede that it does not seem like a great distance. Indeed Jesus walked virtually everywhere He went during His ministry. However, when considering the distance, we dare not forget that the journey was being undertaken by a man who had gone for at least twenty-four hours with little or no sleep, had endured a tumultuous night of grief in prayer, and had endured already that morning multiple severe beatings and a devastating flagellation.

Finally we must consider both the time of day and season in which Jesus carried His burden to Calvary. Yes, it was early in the morning, but not so early as to cause the streets to be empty. Add to that scenario the grapevine effect of the fast-spreading news that this man who had healed an untold number, fed people by the thousands, and even, reportedly, raised people from the dead had been sentenced for execution. The streets were crowded with people standing, looking on in amazement.

So now there is a broader picture of Jesus carrying His one-hundred-pound *patibulum*, His arms outstretched and tied across the length of it, stumbling through a densely crowded city to the place of His execution. The weight of that burden digging into the exposed muscles of His shoulders left marks that we see on the shroud.

Pierced in His hands and feet

When Jesus was placed on the cross, nails were driven through His hands and feet. We read in John 20:25–27:

> The other disciples therefore said to him, "We have seen the Lord."
>
> So [Thomas] said to them, "Unless I see in His hands the print of the nails, and put my finger into the print of the nails, and put my hand into His side, I will not believe."
>
> And after eight days His disciples were again inside, and Thomas with them. Jesus came, the doors being shut, and stood in the midst, and said, "Peace to you!" Then He said to Thomas, "Reach your finger here, and look at My hands;

and reach your hand here, and put it into My side. Do not be unbelieving, but believing."

The wounds in Jesus's hands were caused by nails that were approximately five to seven inches long. They were driven through the wrists and into the wood of the crossbeam. These nails, again, placed through the wrists would have caused massive destruction to the median nerve in the wrists. This would have caused the hand to be frozen in an open fist. The wounds in the feet were from similar but longer nails driven through the feet into an extended footrest, called a *suppedaneum*.

The wound in the side

It was the custom, in order to hasten the death of the condemned, to break the legs of crucified men. This act prevented the men from raising themselves up in order to gasp great lungfuls of air. The Bible says that when the soldier approached Jesus, it was noted that He, Jesus, was already dead. The Bible says in John 19:32–34:

> Then the soldiers came and broke the legs of the first and of the other who was crucified with Him. But when they came to Jesus and saw that He was already dead, they did not break His legs. But one of the soldiers pierced His side with a spear, and immediately blood and water came out.

This mixture conforms to Bucklin's findings.

HOW DID THE IMAGE APPEAR?

There have been many theories regarding the process through which the image, whatever it is, could have been made. However, in testing these theoretical models, most fail.

Science says that the image could not have been caused by decomposition. This is easy enough to understand, as there is no image left on the lining of coffins. Additionally we know that in whatever way the body left the shroud, the cloth itself was undisturbed. We know that the shroud is stained with type AB blood, but the body appears to have been pushed through the material of the cloth.

Since 1978 STURP (Shroud of Turin Research Project, many of whose members are atheists or agnostics; all are scientists, none preachers or evangelists) has produced interesting findings. It has been determined that any DNA processing from the shroud would be impossible, as the blood has been so contaminated with the tears shed over it across the centuries. But there is particular pollen that is cause for amazement. Professor Avinoam Danin, a botanist with the Hebrew University of Jerusalem, "has confirmed that of the hundreds of floral patterns on the sheet (i.e. shroud), 28 are of flower species that still grow in Israel, 70 percent of them in a 10-square kilometer area between Jerusalem and Jericho. At least one of them, Zygophyllum (Dumosum), a kind of desert tumbleweed (actually a shrub), grows only in Israel and parts of neighboring Jordan and Sinai, as it did 2,000 years ago in the time of Jesus."[18]

Many of these pollens come from flowers that, Danim says, would have been consistent with the Jewish burial practice of ringing the head of the deceased with flowers. Additionally the majority of identified species were used medicinally as body preservatives.

Danim also says that of the twenty-eight flower species identified on the shroud, 96 percent of them grow between Jerusalem and the Qumran caves. When we factor in the southern Dead Sea area to the equation, 100 percent of the species can be found. Danim goes on to say, "I can't say for certain that it was Jesus's shroud. But this evidence backs up the possibility that it is genuine, and there is no doubt that it comes from the Land of Israel."[19]

Finally, I want to linger on the pollen to take note of one very particular flower. The *capperis aegyptia* is a peculiar flower in that it only opens and sheds pollen from three to four o'clock in the afternoon between the months of January and April!

Photographic evidence

It is important to note that although through the centuries the shroud was believed to be the burial cloth of Jesus, the image we have come to associate with it was not visible in the way we understand it. Plainly put, the image of the man that we see today was not visible to us before May of 1898. You see, while the shroud was on display in Turin, an amateur photographer by the name of Secondo Pia took a picture of the relic. During the course of developing the photographic plates, Pia saw the unmistakable image of a man. The image he saw in the negative looked like a positive photographic image.[20] This is significant, because it causes us to understand that the image on the shroud is a reversal of normal visual convention. In normal photos we see with light highlights and dark shadows, but on the shroud, that process is reversed.

Almost a century after the photograph was taken, in 1976, the image was studied at the Sandia National Laboratory and rendered using a computer called a VP8 Image Analyzer. This computer could convert image intensity to vertical relief. In short, a flat image from the shroud was used to produce a 3D model. What the analysts found was that the relief image was anatomically correct for a human body, even down to the subtle details of the face. This remained true to further renderings of the body.[21]

How Did the Body Get Out?

The most notable aspect of the appearance of this image on the fabric of the shroud is this: the image could not have been preserved in the way it was if human hands had unwrapped the body and removed it from the cloth itself. The image would have distorted and warped in the unrolling. I will not go too deep into the scientific aspect of this for the simple reason that volumes of books have been written on this subject, and I have only a couple of pages. But let me give the most stunning evidence.

A paper coauthored by attorney and historian Mark Antonacci

and physicist Arthur Lind makes the case that the image of the crucified man in the Shroud of Turin may represent a kind of photograph taken at the instant Jesus's body transformed as He rose from the dead. In their paper "Particle Radiation From the Body" their argument focuses on twenty-nine distinctive features that various scientists have found of the four decades of study of the shroud's image and fibers. Among these are a lack of image diminishment, uniform coloring on the linen, oxidation and dehydration of the same, equal intensity on frontal and dorsal views, as well as the aforementioned photographic and pollinic evidence.[22]

The conclusion reached by Antonacci is that "all of these features can be accounted for by radiation and only radiation will account for all of them."[23] The assertion is that only radiation or light coming from within the body would explain all of these occurrences. What this means is that, according to Antonacci, "the source of light does not originate outside of the body, the cloth, or the tomb, but with the body itself. The weave of the inner part of the cloth containing the frontal and dorsal images is not even part of the distinctive images, which they too, would have been, if the light came from anywhere outside the body."[24]

Interestingly their research even accounts for the findings of the 3D model created by the VP8 Image Analyzer. They ask:

> What if the man's body became insubstantial or dematerialized instantly leaving behind some energy in the form of the basic particles of matter, such as protons, neutrons and electromagnetic waves, such as gamma rays?[25]

The simple answer is that if this is indeed how the resurrection physically occurred, then the part of the cloth closest to the body would have received the most radiation, while the part farthest away would have received the least. This would have caused "true three-dimensional information being encoded onto the two-dimensional cloth," and this is exactly what we find on the shroud.

In his book *The Resurrection of the Shroud*, Antonacci states, "If a body instantaneously dematerialized or disappeared, particle radiation would be given off naturally and all the unique features found on the Shroud's body images and blood marks would occur."[26] He goes on to say that "for either ionizing particles or neutrons to have irradiated the Shroud from a corpse would have been an unprecedented event that could only be explained by the resurrection."[27]

THE MYSTERY REVEALED

Much like the mystery of the ark of the covenant, the Shroud of Turin and all of the information that it holds for us are witness to the truth. It is again truth that has sprung from the ground. But why?

I believe that God knew there would be skeptics. There are those among us who are always (if not overly) analytical, always asking questions. They demand proof. They want something they can actually touch. The shroud is yet another evidence of the superiority of Christianity over Islam, Buddhism, Judaism, and any other "leader-centric" religion, because the God we serve is alive today, and we have physical proof! We have a witness to His greatness!

Remember that there are "three that bear witness in heaven" (1 John 5:7) of our salvation. But it is not just there. There are "three that bear witness on earth: the Spirit, the water, and the blood; and these three agree as one" (v. 8). The Spirit who was sent as our "helper" bears witness not only to our salvation but also to His enduring love for us. The waters of baptism bear witness to the death of our selves and to the new life we have been given in Christ. The blood on the ark bears witness to Jesus's suffering and sacrificial perfection, and the blood on the shroud bears witness to His triumph over the grave! On a face cloth in Oviedo, Spain, and on a shroud in Turin, Italy, there is blood evidence that Jesus of Nazareth is Lord of Hosts!

Chapter 16

The MYSTERY *of the* CHURCH

L ET'S GO TO church!"
"Hey! Welcome to church!"
"What church do you want to go to this week?"

I have heard those phrases and others like them (and even said them) all of my life. And, with no condemnation toward myself or any who use them, it is time for their use to end.

The word *church* comes from two words in the original Greek: *ek*, meaning "from out of," and *kaleo*, meaning "to call." So this word *church* indicates those who have been called out of something. The current concept of buildings, institutions, and even programs as "the church" is a gross error. Buildings, institutions, denominations, and the like are servants of the church, but they are not *the* church. Of the hundreds of references to the church in the Bible, only two refer to a local assembly of people.

This local assembly manifests itself under three figures of speech in the Book of Ephesians: the church is called a bride, a building, and a body. This wonderful fellowship we call a church is, according to Ephesians 5:32, a divine mystery. When we search the writings of the New Testament, we discover that Israel was set aside due to their rejection of Jesus. But then, from both Jew and Gentile, God created a new people. Ephesians 3 declares that this new body of people was a mystery.

In Ephesians 3:2–6 we read:

> You have heard of the dispensation of the grace of God which was given to me for you, how that by revelation He made known to me the mystery (as I have briefly written already, by which, when you read, you may understand my knowledge in the mystery of Christ), which in other ages was not made known to the sons of men, as it has now been revealed by the Spirit to His holy apostles and prophets: that the Gentiles should be fellow heirs, of the same body, and partakers of His promise in Christ through the gospel.

Later in verse 9 of the same chapter, Paul writes that this revelation is "to make all see what is the fellowship of the mystery, which from the beginning of the ages has been hidden in God who created all things through Jesus Christ." What we discover in these few verses is that Paul is in the process of explaining a mystery that was not known before his time, but it was in God's heart from before the beginning of time.

You see, the church is a group of people gathered together in Christ. Whether that gathering is in an old storefront, a hut in the jungle, someone's home, or a large cathedral is irrelevant. The church was not an afterthought by God; the church was the secret surprise God had in store for humanity all along.

ECCLESSIA

There is a theology destroying the church that I first noticed when I read the works of Cyrus I. Scofield. Scofield and others taught through dispensationalist that God intended for the Jews to accept Jesus as their Messiah. Subsequent to their rejection of Jesus, God had to do something, and so He created the church. This is simply not true.

It is important to note that all of this talk of a mysterious body called the church is couched within a particular section of Ephesians in which Paul was discussing marriage and family. In Ephesians 5:31–33 Paul wrote:

"For this reason a man shall leave his father and mother and be joined to his wife, and the two shall become one flesh." *This is a great mystery*, but I speak concerning Christ and the church. Nevertheless let each one of you in particular so love his own wife as himself, and let the wife see that she respects her husband.

—EMPHASIS ADDED

It is not marriage or family that is the mystery. It is no mystery for a man to leave father and mother to get married. *The mystery is Christ and the church.* The mystery of Jesus Christ leaving the heavenly Father to come to the earth for His bride and companion is beautifully figured in Genesis 2. Adam is put to sleep, and from his side is taken a rib from which woman is made. The Lord Jesus was put to death, and from His bleeding side there came the church. You see, just as Eve was "in Adam" all the time, we, the church, were in Christ from eternity. Ephesians 1:6 states that we are "accepted in the Beloved," and as Jesus is the "Beloved Son," I was accepted in Him before the world was created.

The woman at Jacob's well pointed out to Jesus that there was contention between Samaritans and Jews over the proper location for worship. Jesus told her that the time had come for a new people to worship in Spirit and truth (John 4:19–24). Later He announced to His disciples that He would build His church upon a confession of faith, not a foundation of stone.

This word *ecclesia* was in the first-century world a political term. It was used in the sense of calling out citizens to an assembly for a vote. There were prerequisites for this privilege. A person had to be a citizen who was free and without a criminal record. This is true of church membership as well. No, I don't mean any of these in a temporal sense.

To be a member of the church you have to be a citizen of heaven. In Philippians 3:20 it says that "our citizenship is in heaven, from which we also eagerly wait for the Savior, the Lord Jesus Christ."

Additionally we are free. In Romans 6:22 we are told that in Christ we have "been set free from sin, and having become slaves of God, you have your fruit to holiness, and the end, everlasting life." Also, remember the great promise from Jesus Himself, when He said:

> Most assuredly, I say to you, whoever commits sin is a slave of sin. And a slave does not abide in the house forever, but a son abides forever. Therefore if the Son makes you free, you shall be free indeed.
>
> —JOHN 8:34–36

And finally, in Romans 3:24 we read that even though we were once guilty of having broken the whole law (see James 2:10), we have now been not simply exonerated but "justified freely by [God's] grace through the redemption that is in Christ Jesus."

What the church is (and is not)

Though we organize for effective service, the church is not an organization. Though we use business concepts to carry on our work, the church is not a business. Instead, the church is, or at the very least should be, a people energized by and operating in the Holy Spirit. Throughout his letters Paul refers to things such as the energy, or working, of God's power (Eph. 3:7; Phil. 3:21) and "striving according to His working [energy] which works in me mightily" (Col. 1:29). This is a reference to God empowering us, through the Holy Spirit, to do more than we ever dreamed we could and more than we are able to do alone.

Many years ago Oswald Chambers attended a World's Fair. A display some distance away from where he stood caught his eye. It was a man pumping furiously, and large volumes of water were coming out of the pump. Never had he seen a man pump so much water. When he got closer, Chambers saw that the man was simply a mannequin and that it was the water driving the pump.[1] When will we learn that God is the power that drives us? He is the source of our energy and operation.

The Work

The church has had an unprecedented opportunity to move three worlds. First, we can affect and shape this present world. In Ephesians 3:6–9 Paul explains that his calling is to preach "the unsearchable riches of Christ" (v. 8) among the Gentiles so that everyone could learn them (v. 9). Evangelism must be the heartbeat of the church. Paul saw this gospel truth as priceless. Witnessing to the lost must be a priority to the church. We are the witness to our world.

The church also has an impact on the supernatural world. In Ephesians 3:10–11 Paul says that the intent of all those "unsearchable riches of Christ" is that the "manifold wisdom of God might be made known by the church to the principalities and powers in the heavenly places." The forces of hell are to be informed through the church of how wise God was in calling out a people for His name. Satan, his minions, and even the foundations of hell themselves should tremble when the church gathers together. In Matthew 16:18 it says that the gates of hell shall not prevail against the church. This picture is not of the forces of hell assaulting the church and being unsuccessful. It is instead a picture of the church storming the very gates of hell and releasing the captives!

The church also bears a significant impact on the world to come. Through our work in this present world, in our work against the forces of darkness, the world to come will be shaped by the people we bring into the church. Paul wrote again in Ephesians 3:20–21:

> Now to Him who is able to do exceedingly abundantly above all that we ask or think, according to the power that works in us, to Him be glory in the church by Christ Jesus *to all generations*, forever and ever. Amen.
>
> —EMPHASIS ADDED

You see, the church of Jesus Christ, God's mysterious fellowship, has the opportunity to win the lost and, in so doing, change the landscape of not only this world but also the world to come.

THE CHURCH AGE

It really would not be appropriate to discuss the mystery of the church and not give mention to the prophecy of the church age given in Revelation. I discussed this at length in a twenty-two-week study of this mysterious book. (The DVD or CD, with my exhaustive study notes and outlines, is available for purchase.) While the last mention of the church in the Bible is in Revelation 22:16, chapters 2–3 of Revelation contain a record of seven historical churches that represent the future history of the church until the present day. They also clearly represent the types of churches that will be on earth at the end. Four of the seven are told to watch for His coming, so we would expect churches like them to be present at the Second Coming.

The other three needed rebuke. The church at Thyatira represents the compromised church. They had allowed a false prophetess to not only enter the church but also to teach and seduce the servants. The church at Sardis was a sleeping church, a church of traditions. Jesus said to them, "I know your works, that you have a name that you are alive, but you are dead" (Rev. 3:1). Finally, the church of Laodicea was the lukewarm church, a church without fire, passion, or energy. To them Jesus said, "I know your works, that you are neither cold nor hot. I could wish you were cold or hot. So then, because you are lukewarm, and neither cold nor hot, I will vomit you out of My mouth" (Rev. 3:15–16).

Only one church will be truly thriving at the end of the age. This will be the Philadelphian church—the church that patiently endured. To them Jesus said:

> These things says He who is holy, He who is true, "He who
> has the key of David, He who opens and no one shuts, and

shuts and no one opens": "I know your works. See, I have set
before you an open door, and no one can shut it; for you have
a little strength, have kept My word, and have not denied My
name....Because you have kept My command to persevere, I
also will keep you from the hour of trial which shall come
upon the whole world, to test those who dwell on the earth."

—REVELATION 3:7–8, 10

This church is given the key of David. This key is Davidic
worship. We are reminded of this in the aforementioned verse,
Revelation 22:16, in which Jesus said, "I, Jesus, have sent My angel
to testify to you these things in the churches. I am the Root and
the Offspring of David, the Bright and Morning Star." When exam-
ining the panorama of Revelation, we see economic collapse with
the fall of Babylon, the failure of man-made harlot religion, war,
famine, disease, near anarchy! It would seem odd that the last thing
Jesus said to the church would include a mention of David. Why
would Jesus do that?

THE DAVIDIC COMPANY

Of all the persons mentioned, described, or chronicled in the pages
of Scripture, there is only one named David, and he was, in many
ways, unlike anybody before or after him. His differences bear
weight in the context of the church as well.

Consider that David looked different. In a dark-skinned culture
David was described as "ruddy, and of a fair countenance" (1 Sam.
17:42, KJV) "with bright eyes" (1 Sam 16:12). His hair was red! His
skin was pale, and he had blue eyes. He was not even recognized as
a son by his own father when the prophet Samuel came looking for
a new king. David was, in a word, different.

Additionally David behaved differently. I have a pastor friend
who always jokingly refers to David as the "one real hippie in the
Bible." David was content to watch the sheep and hang out in the

fields. David wrote poetry and played his guitar while he sang and danced before God under the stars.

David could fight. He was an expert soldier. When he was still a young boy, he had killed at least one lion, at least one bear, and a nine-foot behemoth named Goliath.

David was also a type of Christ. Recall that at the baptism of Jesus, the skies opened and God was heard to say, "This is My beloved Son" (Matt. 3:17). The word *beloved* in Hebrew is *Dahveed*, or David. This Davidic connection with Jesus is reinforced at Jesus's triumphal entry into Jerusalem. In Mark 11:9–11 we read that the worshipers cried out:

> Hosanna! "Blessed is He who comes in the name of the LORD!" Blessed is the kingdom of our father David that comes in the name of the Lord! Hosanna in the highest!

All of this is true for the church as well. The church is called to look different from those outside of it. I am not talking about dress or hairstyles or jewelry but about a possession of a Holy Spirit fire that changes our appearance from the inside out. The church must look different, act differently, be willing to fight, and be full of passionate worshippers.

THE MYSTERY REVEALED

The mystery of the church is greater than these pages can contain, but the truth behind the mystery is simple and clear: God loves you! When He looks down at us, we are not different races, different genders, different classes, and all of those trappings that we tend to focus on. In the first Adam the human race was divided into different races, skin colors, languages, and such. We are all, in our flesh, off from what we were meant to be. In Tennessee English, "We ain't right!" It's just that simple.

If you look at yourself and think that this is what a human being is supposed to be, you might as well go to a junkyard, find a rusted-out, wrecked Lamborghini, and think that that's what a high-performance automobile is. This body that you are in is the last remnant of Adam subject to the fall, but it is not who you are! You are not defined by whether your skin is dark or light, by whether you have hair or no hair, by being a man or woman, or even by your national origin. Just as Adam was the federal head of the human race, so the second Adam, Jesus Christ, is the federal head of a new race of people called the church! The only part of that we do not yet have is our glorified body.

You see, if you are still looking around and noticing differences in people, you are not seeing the church. The mystery of the church is that in Christ all of our differences disappear, and we are brought together in unity to worship the King and to do His work. Understanding that, we become aware that in Christ, Baptists and Pentecostals, people with dark skin and people with light skin, rich and poor, male and female, Jew and Gentile, Iranian and Israeli, are able to see past any human difference and see the great witness of the blood that washes over us and makes us one in Christ.

Chapter 17

The MYSTERY *of* HOLY SPIRIT FULLNESS

I HAVE SPOKEN AT some length about the Holy Spirit and the life of the Christian. This placement of the Holy Spirit is called the anointing. It, like everything else we are discussing here, is a mystery. In Colossians 1:26–27 Paul wrote:

> [The fulfillment of the word of God is] the mystery which has been hidden from ages and from generations, but now has been revealed to His saints. To them God willed to make known what are the riches of the glory of this mystery among the Gentiles: which is Christ in you, the hope of glory.

Here this phrase "Christ in you" is found. But just as importantly we see again that this word *mystery* is used to indicate not something hidden but something that God is revealing. Paul said that the mystery "has been hidden from ages." Yes, it was at one point not revealed, because Messiah had to come for these mysteries to be revealed. So what do we mean here by the mystery of the Spirit?

A SACRED SECRET

In his letter to the Colossians, Paul points out that the hidden treasures of God are hidden in Christ Jesus. All the mysteries of the Bible are sacred secrets that are available to every believer. Colossians 1:26 says that the mystery has been revealed "to [God's] saints." That word *saints* simply means "holy ones." This does not mean holy in the sense that the word is so often used but simply that the saints are ones whom God has set apart.

Salvation—being "born again," being "reborn," being "converted," being "washed in the blood," "getting saved," or whatever term you might be prone to use—is a wonderful experience with the Holy Spirit. The church, however, has done a great disservice to the world. We have tried to tell people that there is a "plan of salvation." We have printed leaflets and tracts, written books and sermons, recorded songs about this "plan." Don't misunderstand me. There *is* a message of salvation. But people have a tendency to think that if we can memorize something that's easy, then that is the route we are going to take. So we tend to take the unbeliever through the "Romans Road." Was that Jesus's witnessing method? No!

There is nothing wrong with knowing the facts and being able to present them, but what we have done is pluck green fruit and brought lost people into the church because they agreed with a plan. But these people were never truly converted! Salvation is a revelation of the Spirit of God and the work He has done in our lives. Jesus Christ literally, in reality, by His Spirit comes to live in our lives. It is not just a process of some prayer and not feeling anything or really knowing anything.

Salvation is a simple yet mysterious truth. The way is clear: a person must agree with God about his sins and turn from them. He must personally invite Jesus into his life as Lord and Savior. My friend Ron Dunn put it best, I think, when he said that salvation happens when "we give all we know about ourselves to all we know about Jesus." This is a transaction that takes place by faith.

Even when put so simply, we must understand that there is an invisible, mysterious, and wonderful change that takes place in the life of the new convert. Salvation is not now, nor has it ever been, simply knowing "the plan of salvation." It is not accepting facts, though facts must be believed.

No! I say again, true conversion is the work of the Holy Spirit. That is the mystery of conversion. God's Spirit moves into our inner person to live in us during our years upon earth. Again it must be more than feeling. I have heard some people say, "You don't have to feel anything." That is simply untrue! The Bible warns us about being past feeling. Salvation is God coming to live in us for the rest of our lives! That is something to get excited about. I am not trying to cast doubt, but God forbid we assume that just because we mouthed a prayer and acknowledged the four spiritual laws that we somehow slipped in without being converted, redeemed, and regenerated by the Spirit in our lives.

In John chapter 3 Jesus was witnessing to a religious man named Nicodemus. Now if Jesus had been to a "Reaching the Lost" seminar at one of our local churches, then He certainly would have sat Nicodemus down with a copy of the Old Testament and said, "Nicodemus, there are four verses you need to know." But that isn't what happened. Jesus told Nicodemus that to see the kingdom of God, to be "saved," one must be born again.

Nicodemus could not embrace this concept. In his limited understanding salvation was all physical: keeping the law and all the commandments, studying the law, performing mitzvahs, etc. It was all about him doing something in the physical. But what Jesus wanted Nicodemus to understand was that there was a spiritual birth that was absolutely necessary. In John 3:8 Jesus said:

> The wind blows where it wishes, and you hear the sound of it, but cannot tell where it comes from and where it goes. So is everyone who is born of the Spirit.

To understand this phrase properly, we have to understand that the word *wind* is, in the Greek, the same word as *spirit*. What Jesus explained to Nicodemus here is that conversion is simple but also profound. Out of heaven will come a wind of the Spirit, and though you might not be able to tell where it came from or where it is going, you will know it when it hits you, and it will change you forever.

Something invisible and mysteriously wonderful happens at

true conversion. The Spirit of God, the same Spirit who empowered Jesus in His earthly ministry, the same Spirit who filled Him again and again to perform works beyond the ability of His human frame, the same Spirit who lit Him from the inside out as He lay wrapped in the grave clothes and pushed Him materially through those linens, yes, the same Spirit who raised Jesus from the dead at our conversion takes up residence in our spirit and makes us new!

Salvation is not something simply admirable; it possesses us and causes us to be a peculiar people. It is not simply understood; it is felt and experienced. When a person acknowledges his sins, confesses them, and trusts the death and resurrection of Christ to save him, he *is saved*. We do not receive a plan; we receive a person. We do not receive truth; we receive the One who said, "I am…the truth" (John 14:6).

REACHES AND RICHES

Look back at Colossians 1. Paul said that his mission was to reveal "the riches of the glory of this mystery among the Gentiles" (v. 27). Now in today's society, and especially in the twenty-first-century church, we tend to make much of Jew and Gentile. But the word *Gentiles* as Paul uses it here does not simply mean "non-Jews." Instead, it implies the word *nations*. So what Paul says essentially is that God has called him to reveal the mystery to every nation. What that means is that there is no one on the face of God's earth beyond the redeeming, transforming power of God's salvation.

One can hear in the church, in the home, in the car, on the street, through radio, television, Internet, printed page, or personal witness. In any and every place, at any and every time, the mysterious power of God can touch lives! There is no home, heart, or hiding place in which God cannot find you, reach into you, convict you, and create in you a clean heart by His Spirit.

When that happens, the new convert enters into an inheritance indescribable. This is one of the truths that remain a mystery: the wealth of the believer. The Bible says that we have received a "treasure in earthen vessels" (2 Cor. 4:7), that we have the "pearl of great price" (Matt. 13:46), which is worth selling all we have to obtain. The truth is that we now possess what money cannot buy and works cannot earn. Our salvation has brought with it, as a free gift from God, inexhaustible abundance.

We read that Jesus said, "I have come that they may have life, and that they may have it more abundantly" (John 10:10). Also, Paul wrote that "God is able to make all grace abound toward you, that you, always having all sufficiency in all things, may have an abundance for every good work" (2 Cor. 9:8) and that God is "able to do exceedingly abundantly above all that we ask or think, according to the power that works in us" (Eph. 3:20). In Christ, according to His Word and by His Spirit, we have abundant life, abundant grace, and abundant power!

We are told that the earth uses only one part in two million of the sun's energy. We have enough energy striking our planet every day to end the energy shortage forever. How sad it is that we cannot harness that power. But in the church we have the same problem. We are not, I think, availing ourselves of God's abundant provision either. We are saved and know the Lord. His wealth is ours! There is no reason for us not to claim it!

I heard a story that several years ago in Chattanooga there was a soup kitchen in operation, and two women were standing in line to receive food. One lady had a half-gallon jug, and the other had a five-gallon bucket. The lady with the smaller jug asked the other, "You don't expect to get that filled, do you?" The other lady replied, "Yes! All they asked was for us to bring a container." How often do we lack because we refuse to recognize the riches we have in Christ?

CHRIST IN ME

I have expounded at length on the wonderful mystery of Christ in us, but it is so great, so wonderful, *and* so far-reaching that it bears further illustration. The message of the Spirit is that Jesus Christ lives in us by the Holy Spirit. We can be baptized in the Spirit, filled with the Spirit, sealed by the Spirit, and can yield fruit of the Spirit. We can pray in the Spirit, live in the Spirit, walk in the Spirit, and abide in the Spirit. We can worship in the Spirit and be set free in the Spirit. We can be anointed by the Spirit and receive the provision of the Spirit. Why? Because Jesus Christ lives in us!

And because of that we are given "the hope of glory" (Col. 1:27). By the Spirit we can, right now, experience the riches of His glory, but, according to the Bible, as much as there might ever be of that experience here on earth, there is yet more to hope for. There remains a "hope." I'll discuss that hope in the next chapter, but how wonderful is it that the abundant life, filled with power and grace with all the riches of Christ that we are able to experience on this side of heaven, is only a taste of the hope to come?

The Mystery Revealed

Bill Cosby once humorously stated that the point of philosophy was to ask the really deep and significant life questions such as "Why is there air?" He made it a joke, but few people know that it took humans thousands of years to prove that air exists, let alone that it was matter. The problem is that the subject of that study was invisible. Scientists could not see the object of their study but had to rely on indirect evidence.

The nebulous state of air has even been used as an analogy to the existence of God. "You can't see the wind," the argument goes, "but you can feel and see its effect. It's the same with God." Now scientifically, yes, that is a shaky argument, but when we think back to Jesus's words to Nicodemus, it seems that the Lord Himself might have jumped on that wagon. Yes, we see the effects of wind, but it is impossible to know where that wind comes from or where it is going. And it is the same with those born of the Spirit.

You see, when the lost world looks at one born of the Spirit, they cannot see what that person has. There is hope in him of future glory; a glory that, though present, is still yet to come. Those born of the Spirit are anchored in heaven already by the anchor rope of hope. The invisible blessed assurance of eternal residence and rank is theirs already.

What we understand is that what is partially enjoyed here will be perfectly enjoyed there. Why? Because Christ's home is heaven. When He took up residence in my life and filled me with His Spirit, heaven became my home too, and now I am homesick for heaven. So it is with everyone born of the Spirit.

It is this work of the Spirit that enables conversion. The one who led me to Christ was probably the worst soul winner in the history of evangelism. This pastor's name was John Bob Riddle. All he ever did was study all day, but his preaching captivated me. I was lost, but my mother begged, pleaded, and pestered him long enough that one day he came to my house and took me for a ride. We talked about God, the sacrifice of Jesus, and salvation, and I was so scared and in such awe of Pastor Riddle that I can barely describe it even now. But he was wise enough not to lead me in a sinner's prayer. He knew I wasn't ready. We got back home, and as I sat in the front seat of his car, he said to me, "Now Brother Ronnie, you're close! But the Holy Spirit will tell you, son. The Holy Spirit will tell you! And when He tells you, you just ask Him! Now go on back inside and tell your mother I talked to you so she'll leave me alone."

I laugh about it now, but three days later as I sat alone on a swing set in the backyard, I couldn't laugh. His words rang over and over in my mind. I had been reading one of my science books (the study of cosmology and such are still my avocation), and I was considering how big the universe was, and suddenly I realized how small I was. I recalled what Pastor John Bob had told me, and I bowed my head and said, "Lord Jesus, Pastor Riddle told me I was a sinner, and I know I am. But I want You to take over my life." And after I prayed, I lay in the grass for an hour looking up at God's creation, and I felt Him as close as the blades of grass that were brushing my face. That is Holy Spirit conversion.

That is not how we do it now. We have plans and programs and seminars and all manner of strategies to bring numbers into the local church, and many pastors and evangelists like to report big numbers—and I praise God for the work that these fine men and women of God do—but true conversion is not about prayers, plans, or numbers. It is about God revealing His Son in us through the Holy Spirit.

The truth of the mystery is that it is no longer a mystery. Christ lives in us here on earth so that we can live with Him in heaven. His wonderful salvation is ours now because of His Spirit.

Chapter 18

The MYSTERY *of the* RAPTURE

A MONG THE UNCONVERTED it is probably the most well known of all Christian teachings. Among the faithful it is probably the most hoped-for moment in history. Among both it is probably the least understood doctrine of the church. The Rapture, that moment when untold numbers of the faithful will somehow disappear from the face of the earth, has been the subject of both secular and faith-based movies and novels. It is a mystery, to be sure, but it is something that we can and should understand.

This is a mystery of the church's future, but it will impact the future of the entire planet, for the church's destiny stretches into eternity future, just as her existence stretches into eternity past. In 1 Corinthians 2:7–9 Paul wrote:

> We speak the wisdom of God in a mystery, the hidden wisdom which God ordained before the ages for our glory, which none of the rulers of this age knew; for had they known, they would not have crucified the Lord of glory.
>
> But as it is written: "Eye has not seen, nor ear heard, nor have entered into the heart of man the things which God has prepared for those who love Him."

It still boggles my mind that in all that I have seen and experienced in all my years on this planet, that in all that I have seen and experienced in my forty-eight years of ministry—the thousands of lives changed through the preaching of the gospel, the reconciliation of marriages, the healings, the victories—my eyes have never seen, my ears have never heard, nor have I even imagined the greatness and multiplicity of what God has in store not just for me but also for any who love Him.

What we have to understand, then, is that if these things that God has for us are not visible to the eye nor even imaginable to us, then the reality of them must exist somewhere beyond this temporal realm. The threshold of that place will be opened at the Rapture.

THE BASICS

Most skeptics cite the fact that the word *rapture* does not appear anywhere in Scripture as plain evidence that it is not a valid teaching. While it is true that the word does not appear in the Bible, we get the word from an understanding of 1 Thessalonians 4:16–17:

> For the Lord Himself will descend from heaven with a shout, with the voice of an archangel, and with the trumpet of God. And the dead in Christ will rise first. Then we who are alive and remain shall be *caught up* together with them in the clouds to meet the Lord in the air. And thus we shall always be with the Lord.
> —EMPHASIS ADDED

The word translated "caught up" in this passage is the Greek word *harpazó*, a verb meaning to seize, catch away, pluck, pull up, or take. This word was translated into the Latin *rapio* in the Vulgate. From this we get the English word *rapture*.

The doctrine of the Rapture is a portion of Christian eschatology (end-times study) that is the first stage of Christ's return. In this stage Jesus will not return physically to earth but will come in such a way that He "takes up," or "snatches away," His bride, the church, to escape a coming time of tribulation. We have a hint of what that experience will be like in the previously mentioned passage of 1 Thessalonians 4. Jesus will descend from heaven and with a "shout" call away every Christian, first the ones who have died and then the ones who are living.

The Great Change

I think part of the reason that the concept of the Rapture is so hard to grasp is that it seems as if it is something straight out of science fiction. As a culture, especially in the West, we have been conditioned over time to think of the idea of people simply disappearing from life as a phenomenon found only in the annals of *Star Trek*, alien-abduction stories, and the like. But the Bible tells us that not only is the Rapture going to happen, but it is also indispensable. In 1 Corinthians 15:50 Paul tells us, "Flesh and blood cannot inherit the kingdom of God; nor does corruption inherit incorruption." Heaven and the glories there are perfect, and we cannot receive the fullness of that inheritance in our earthly bodies.

The body we live in is sinful. Even as converted, changed saints saved by grace, with every sin put under the blood, we live in a corrupted version of the body God intended for us. We rest in God's inheritance, while we struggle with Adam's curse. Paul later alludes to this in 2 Corinthians 5:2–3 when he says:

> For in this we groan, earnestly desiring to be clothed with our habitation which is from heaven, if indeed, having been clothed, we shall not be found naked.

Paul says that there will come a time when we will receive special "clothing" from heaven that will cover the nakedness of our corruption.

I can hear the response now: "Wait a minute, Pastor Ron; Jesus had a physical body after the resurrection, and He ascended into heaven!" That is true. But something happened to Jesus's body at the moment of His resurrection. I have already discussed the findings of the Shroud of Turin and that light that transported Jesus at the cellular level out of the shroud. I believe that event was God the

Father changing Jesus's earthly body into a glorified one, a body that was probably the same kind of body that Adam and Eve initially had before the Fall. This was a gift to Jesus, and it will be to us as well. We will need this gift.

In his letter to the Ephesian church, Paul spoke about the gifts God intended to bestow on us. In chapter 1 he wrote:

> [God has] made known to us the mystery of His will, according to His good pleasure which He purposed in Himself, that in the dispensation of the fullness of the times He might gather together in one all things in Christ, both which are in heaven and which are on earth—in Him. In Him also we have obtained an inheritance, being predestined according to the purpose of Him who works all things according to the counsel of His will, that we who first trusted in Christ should be to the praise of His glory.
>
> In Him you also trusted, after you heard the word of truth, the gospel of your salvation; in whom also, having believed, you were sealed with the Holy Spirit of promise, who is the guarantee of our inheritance until the redemption of the purchased possession, to the praise of His glory.
>
> —EPHESIANS 1:9–14

In this passage we see that the mystery being revealed is the destiny of the church. Verse 10 speaks about a great gathering together of all who are in Christ, both in heaven and on earth. Understand that according to God's will, you and I were predestined for this purpose. We can be safe in its promise, because we belong to Christ. By His divine authority He will call for us, and the laws of nature and gravity will be suspended, and we will leave this earth to be with our Savior.

THE VICTORY

The greatest aspect of this is that the Rapture, that moment of change from a temporal body to an eternal, glorified one, is the final sign of the victory we have in Christ. The Rapture is the funeral of death. In 1 Corinthians 15:53–57 Paul says:

> For this corruptible must put on incorruption, and this mortal must put on immortality. So when this corruptible has put on incorruption, and this mortal has put on immortality, then shall be brought to pass the saying that is written: "Death is swallowed up in victory."
>
> "O Death, where is your sting? O Hades, where is your victory?"
>
> The sting of death is sin, and the strength of sin is the law. But thanks be to God, who gives us the victory through our Lord Jesus Christ.

The word *victory* is used three times here. In verse 54 we learn that at the Rapture death will be "swallowed up." This is an aorist verb indicating that it has happened once and for all. Death will forever be a thing of the past.

Jesus demonstrated this with His own resurrection. Death tried to swallow Him, but the grave could not hold Him, and corruption could not even touch Him. In His victory of death and the grave, we see our future. In His empty tomb He left the terror of death forever. Not only is death swallowed up, but the fear of it is also no longer an issue! Jesus's glorious conquest of death and the grave will be manifested in the moment of rapture and resurrection. We will be caught up in the air to be with Him!

When that happens, there will be a great coronation. Paul continues in 1 Corinthians 15:58, saying, "Therefore, my beloved brethren, be steadfast, immovable, always abounding in the work of the Lord, knowing that your labor is not in vain in the Lord." No, our labor is not in vain. The trials and tribulations we suffer here are not for nothing, nor are they forever, nor are they fruitless.

A blessed time of fellowship, communion, examination, and enthronement will occur when we meet Jesus in the air. We will stand before the judgment seat to receive the crowning of our work.

It will then be our great pleasure to cast those crowns at our Lord's feet. Do not misunderstand this. I have heard some say that this is a teasing gift Jesus gives us, because He will then demand it back; I have heard others say that it is a sign of thanklessness to take His gift and then cast it at His feet. No, they misunderstand the dynamic of this moment. Jesus showers His love on us, and we shower our love on Him by acknowledging that He alone is King and by admitting that without Him, the works we did to receive those crowns would have been wasted. He alone is to be praised!

THE BRIDE

To truly understand the concept of the Rapture, it helps to look back into history and study the Jewish wedding ritual of Jesus's day. At every wedding there were three categories of people: the groom, the bride, and the guests. But the wedding was not an occasion without pomp and circumstance, mystery and ritual.

Every Jewish wedding began long before the event with the betrothal. A young man, or his family, would approach a young woman's father with a prepared contract or covenant. This contract outlined several things: who the groom was, what his expectations of the bride were, the promises he made to the bride and her family, etc. Primarily the contract showed the groom's willingness to care for and provide for his bride. The most important element of any contract was the bride price. This was what the young man was willing to pay to marry the young woman. The would-be groom made this payment, which was usually quite high, to the bride's father in exchange for the father's permission to marry the young woman. This might seem callous, but consider two factors:

1. In that culture sons were more valued than daughters, because they could share in more of the work, so the cost incurred raising a daughter was quite high.

2. But more importantly the amount of money was significant in that it showed that the groom had invested himself in the young woman already. He had given his time and work, possibly months or even years, to the attainment of this bride price. The young man was showing that the bride was very valuable and precious to him.

All of this communication happened with the potential bride present. If the bride price was agreeable to the father, and the father approved of the young man, the young woman's father would pour a cup of wine and set it on the table. Now imagine the tension: the young man has come pleading, his entire life savings before him, the father has approved...but now it is all up to the young woman. Would she drink from the cup? If so, she showed her willingness to marry the man. If not, well, I am sure tears were shed even by strong Jewish boys back then.

If the wine was taken, the man and woman were at that moment betrothed. It is important to note that this was not an engagement as we understand it today. This was not a thing easily broken. The betrothal was legally binding, just as if it were a marriage. The one distinction was that the marriage was not consummated.

After this ceremony the groom would disappear. A typical betrothal period was one to two years. During this time the bride and groom would prepare for marriage and generally would not see each other. The groom would, however, continuously send gifts to his bride while they were parted. This showed not only an appreciation of the bride but also was a taste of what he was preparing for her and was intended to help her remember him during the long absence of betrothal.

While he was apart from his bride, the groom would prepare both a wedding chamber for the honeymoon and a place for them to live together. The wedding chamber was typically built onto the bridegroom's father's house or on that property. It was meant to be beautiful and enticing and, notably, had to be built to his father's specifications. After the wedding the bride and groom spent seven days in that room together. The young man could go get his bride only when his father approved.

During this betrothal time the bride was kept in a constant state of *mikveh*, or "ceremonial cleanliness." She was to be set apart. If she went out in public, she wore a veil so that others would know she was betrothed. The bride and her attendants would purchase cosmetics, and the bride would learn to apply them to make herself even more beautiful for the bridegroom. She had to always be ready, because she did not know when the bridegroom might come. It was not uncommon for the groom to come in the middle of the night. The bride's sisters or bridesmaids would be there constantly waiting with her, keeping their candles lit so that both bride and groom would have light.

When the groom's father approved of the wedding chamber, he would send his son to get the bride. The groom would walk, sometimes alone, sometimes with friends, through the streets to his bride's home. He or his friends would blow the shofar, a ram's horn, on the way, announcing their coming.

The groom and bride would escape to the wedding chamber and consummate their marriage. When the deed was first done, the groom would whisper to his friend through the door, who would announce it to the guests, and seven days of feasting and celebration would occur until the bride and groom emerged from their chamber.

Now this was a long explanation, but it is all extremely vital to understanding not only the Rapture but also the sequence of events that will happen during the time of the Tribulation.

You see, Jesus is the groom. He has provided a bride price for us: His own precious blood. When we take the cup of His communion, we announce our willingness to be His bride. Jesus left to go prepare a place for us (John 14:2) so that we could be with Him. While He is gone, He has sent us gifts by His Holy Spirit that give us a small taste of the fortune we have in Him but that also empower us to endure the wait. One day the Father will tell Jesus, "Go and get them!" (See 1 Thessalonians 4:13-17). And Jesus will descend with the sounding of a mighty shofar and the voice of His lieutenant and say, "Come forth!" At that moment we will leave this earthly desolation and be transformed into His proper bride. We will feast at the marriage supper of the Lamb with Him not for a mere seven days but for seven years, while those left on earth are judged and a last remnant is pulled into the kingdom. After those seven years we will emerge with Jesus and watch as He completes His plan of salvation and re-creation.

THE MYSTERY REVEALED

When Jesus stood at the tomb of Lazarus, He wept. "Jesus wept" (John 11:35). That is the shortest verse in all the Bible. I have often wondered why Jesus wept. He had already said that His intent in going to Bethany was to raise Lazarus from the dead. So it isn't that the death of His friend was a surprise.

I think it is easy enough to say that Jesus was experiencing deep compassion with the other mourners present. The compassionate heart of God is evident throughout Scripture. I think it is fair to say that Jesus was weeping over the tragedy of sin. Lazarus, none of us, are meant for death, but our sin consigns us to the grave. I also think it is fair to say that the death of Lazarus, a wealthy and well-known citizen, would have been noticed by many prominent and important people in nearby Jerusalem, and Jesus, by performing this miracle, was essentially signing His own death warrant.

But none of these really hit home for me. I think Jesus was hurting for all of these things, but also most poignantly for the fact that, by raising Lazarus from the dead, He, Jesus, was simultaneously ripping Lazarus from paradise and consigning him to another physical death. As I said before, death is not a state Jesus wants for us. We are made for heaven and eternity.

The moment of translation, the Rapture, will be two things: it will be a clarion call that the gospel is true, and it will be a joke for those who refuse to believe. But make no mistake—it will happen. Why? Because Jesus loves us so much that He simply refuses to allow us to wallow in the mire of this fallen, corrupted planet. He has something better for us. He has something eternal for us. And there is only one way we can receive it: not in these bodies of corruption but in the glorified state of Christ, with the glorified bodies of our own resurrection.

Chapter 19

The MYSTERY *of* ISRAEL'S SURVIVAL

THROUGHOUT THE MILLENNIA of history one people has stood in stark contrast to the rest of the world. This group, through their presence, persecution, and perpetuity, stand as strong evidence of the divine inspiration of Scripture. I can think of no better way to begin this chapter and the question we face than by citing the words of one of America's greatest writers, Mark Twain.

In the late winter of 1898 Twain was living in Austria, having settled there in 1896. After witnessing vicious government-sanctioned anti-Semitism spread from neighboring Czechoslovakia and seeing Vienna's Jews fall victim to political and physical attacks, Twain penned an article entitled "Stirring Times in Austria," which was published in *Harper's Magazine* in March of 1898. The article generated a mountain of response, but it was one letter by an American Jewish lawyer that caught Twain's eye. In it the lawyer asked, "Will you kindly tell me why, in your judgment, the Jews have thus ever been, and are even now, in these days of supposed intelligence, the butt of baseless, vicious animosities?"[1] Twain penned a response essay, also published by *Harper's Magazine*, which was entitled "Concerning the Jews." In it he wrote the following:

> If the statistics are right, the Jews constitute but one per cent. of the human race. It suggests a nebulous dim puff of star dust lost in the blaze of the Milky Way. Properly the Jew ought hardly to be heard of; but he is heard of, has always been heard of. He is as prominent on the planet as any other people, and

his commercial importance is extravagantly out of proportion to the smallness of his bulk. His contributions to the world's list of great names in literature, science, art, music, finance, medicine, and abstruse learning are also away out of proportion to the weakness of his numbers.

He has made a marvelous fight in the world, in all the ages; and has done it with his hands tied behind him. He could be vain of himself, and be excused for it. The Egyptian, the Babylonian, and the Persian rose, filled the planet with sound and splendor, then faded to dream-stuff and passed away; the Greek and the Roman followed, and made a vast noise, and they are gone; other peoples have sprung up and held their torch high for a time, but it burned out, and they sit in twilight now, or have vanished.

The Jew saw them all, beat them all, and is now what he always was, exhibiting no decadence, no infirmities of age, no weakening of his parts, no slowing of his energies, no dulling of his alert and aggressive mind. All things are mortal but the Jew; all other forces pass, but he remains. What is the secret of his immortality?[2]

Indeed what is the secret of the immortality of the Jewish people?

Paul calls the purpose of God for the Jewish nation a mystery. In Romans 11:25 he wrote:

> For I do not desire, brethren, that you should be ignorant of this mystery, lest you should be wise in your own opinion, that blindness in part has happened to [them] until the fullness of the Gentiles has come in.

Though a Jew himself, Paul, upon receiving his place as an apostle, was sent to the Gentiles. Some say that Paul decided to evangelize the Gentile world only after rejection by his Jewish brothers. The dejected Paul, they say, was offended by his lack of success with the Jews. This is simply not true. In fact, Paul was filled with sorrow for his people. He even wrote of his desire to go to hell, losing his salvation for eternity, if it meant the Jews would accept Christ. In Romans 9:1–4 Paul wrote:

> I tell the truth in Christ, I am not lying, my conscience also bearing me witness in the Holy Spirit, that I have great sorrow and continual grief in my heart. For I could wish that I myself were accursed from Christ for my brethren, my countrymen according to the flesh, who are Israelites, to whom pertain the adoption, the glory, the covenants, the giving of the law, the service of God, and the promises.

There are Jews who are saved and being saved at this moment, but the vast majority of Jews are in blindness of unbelief. Nationally they are in deep trouble. Those who would annihilate that nation are all around them. A rising tide of anti-Semitism is sweeping the world. As I write this book, Syria and Iran are prepared to go to war against the Jews. National Socialism (the Nazi movement of Germany) is on the rise in the EU and even here in the United States—from the bloggers who refer to the United States with the epithet "the United States of Israel"[3] to corporate news pundits actively defacing pro-Israel ad[4] to leaders at the upper level of our executive branch flatly ignoring a meeting request from the prime minister—our citizens have begun to drift away from solidarity with their most trusted ally in that region.

Who can forget the Holocaust? The images of emaciated bodies piled haphazardly in the concentration camps of Dachau and Buchenwald; the mass grave from the Bergen-Belsen camp; and the starving and barely clothed prisoners found in late spring behind the gates of the Mauthausen concentration camp still haunt me. Once upon a time Holocaust denial was relegated to extremist neo-Nazi or white-supremacist movements. Today internationally respected world leaders build anti-Semitic and anti-Western platforms that hinge on the denial of the Holocaust. In 2008 a

University of Haifa survey showed that 40.5 percent of Israeli Arabs deny that the Holocaust actually occurred.[5]

Now I believe that we should support a Jewish state, but not simply because of the Holocaust, but I bring it up as an illustration. The Zionist movement was in full swing long before World War II, but it was the Holocaust that solidified the global view that the Jewish people needed a place where they could be safe. The denial of the Holocaust and the attempt to convince others that it did not exist is not simply an attack on the Jewish people; it is also an attack on that cornerstone of the need for them to exist.

But is that all there is? Should we support a continuing Jewish state just to lower the chances of a future holocaust? No! Absolutely not! Additionally, just as we have pointed to other physical evidence as a great testimony to the truth of the Word of God, so the continued, unstoppable existence of the Jewish people is proof of the same.

THE MYSTERIOUS PAST

There is usually an assumption that the Jewish people were magically birthed with the calling of Abraham. This is not the case. Long before they were called Jews, or Israelites, they were referred to as "Hebrews." This term comes from Shem, the son of Noah. He was called in Genesis 10:21 "the father of all the children of Eber." Abraham was the great-great-great-great grandson of Eber, and even four generations removed, Eber lived for two hundred years after the birth of Abraham. Remember as well that Abraham himself was only sixty-nine years old when Noah died. Noah's father talked to Adam, and Abraham actually spoke to Noah.

After the Flood the family of Shem populated the area of modern-day Iran and Iraq. The ruins of Ur are two hundred twenty miles southeast of Baghdad. The excavation of that city is still visible. It was a wealthy city. According to C. L. Woolley in his book *Abraham: Recent Discoveries and Hebrew Origins*, the worship of the city god of Ur, the moon god Nannar, and Nannar's consort Ningal was big business. Woolley describes in minute detail the sacred temples of the city in which were the famous ziggurat and the various buildings erected to the moon god and his consort, with a description of the moon god ritual. The family of Abraham (then Abram) was a big part of that business. God called Abram out of that city, out of that country, and away from his family to a new land (Gen. 12:1–3).

We are not told why God chose this particular branch of the family. God's motives remain a mystery. Deuteronomy 7:7 says that "the Lord did not set His love on you nor choose you because you were more in number than any other people, for you were the least of all peoples." And yet it is also clear that Abraham's descendants were chosen as a special people in the earth above all people. They were not special in themselves, but God's choice made them special. They were to be a people through whom He would speak to His world and through whom He would come into the world.

Israel was not more righteous than other nations. I have heard some preachers teach that the reason God gave the Promised Land to the Hebrews was because they had shown themselves to be righteous. But in Deuteronomy 9:6 we read that such was not the case at all. It reads:

> Therefore understand that the Lord your God is not giving
> you this good land to possess because of your righteousness,
> for you are a stiff-necked people.

No, it was God's love and His sovereign choice that gave the land and the covenants to the people of Israel.

Ultimately God did not give the land to the Jews in Deuteronomy, just prior to their entrance into the land. No, the land had already been given unconditionally to Abraham back in Genesis 15:18–21, where we read:

On the same day the LORD made a covenant with Abram, saying:

"To your descendants I have given this land, from the river of Egypt to the great river, the River Euphrates—the Kenites, the Kenezzites, the Kadmonites, the Hittites, the Perizzites, the Rephaim, the Amorites, the Canaanites, the Girgashites, and the Jebusites.

Over one hundred forty Old Testament passages confirm that the land was given to the children of Abraham.

THE PRIVILEGED CHILD

God's special choice of Israel granted to them certain privileges. In the last section I alluded to two of them, but in Romans 9:4–5 the apostle Paul cited the litany. He wrote:

[To the] Israelites…pertain the adoption, the glory, the covenants, the giving of the law, the service of God, and the promises; of whom are the fathers and from whom, according to the flesh, Christ came, who is over all, the eternally blessed God. Amen.

This is quite a list. What are these promises?

Adoption

For the most part we do not understand adoption the way the word is used in the Bible. In America and other first-world countries, adoption is usually seen as a good deed or even as a ministry of love. It is those things. However, the first-century mind would have understood the term *adoption* far more solemnly than we, generally speaking, do.

Understand that the adopted child was not considered adopted in the sense that he or she was somehow inferior or even different from the biological children of the family. The adopted child had every right and privilege that his siblings did. When he came of age, the adopted child could enter into business in the name of his family. This does not seem so odd to us, but it is important to understand that a biological child whose paternity was suspect might not have had these same privileges. Additionally it is important to note that often there would be a special gift given to the adopted child out of the family inheritance. But the most important aspect in understanding adoption in the first-century mind is this: the child of the adopted child was considered blood kin to the rest of the family.

When we consider adoption, we are led to understand the science of grafting. In Romans 11:17 Paul wrote of the Christian:

> Some of the branches were broken off, and you, being a wild
> olive tree, were grafted in among them, and with them became
> a partaker of the root and fatness of the olive tree.

The very process of grafting is joining a desirable stem or bud of one plant (the scion) onto the less desirable but hardier stem of another (the stock). This gives a stronger root system than the scion normally would have had. The point, however, is that when the flesh of that scion attaches to the stock, the two intermingle in such a way that it can become almost impossible to determine where one begins and the other ends. So it is with physical adoption. Adoption in God's mind is not bringing a child into your home and caring for it only. Instead, adoption is a grafting in of one (or, in the case of Abraham, a lineage) who is not your own into yourself in such a way that it becomes impossible to extricate the scion from the stock.

Such was the privilege given to Israel. Called out of obscurity, given special place among all the peoples of the world, and gifted with a land for eternity, the Israelites rose out of orphanhood and received a particular adoption from God.

Glory

The Shekinah, or the dwelling presence of God, first came into the earth when it dwelt among the Israelites in the wilderness. We must be very careful in understanding this fact. The Shekinah is not an abstract idea. It is not, as some claim, akin to Sophia, or wisdom, as understood in fringe Christian or even New Age movements. The Shekinah is the literal presence of God. Exodus 40:34–35 tells us:

> Then the cloud covered the tabernacle of meeting, and the glory of the LORD filled the tabernacle. And Moses was not able to enter the tabernacle of meeting, because the cloud rested above it, and the glory of the LORD filled the tabernacle.

This was a heavy and abiding presence, not simply a good feeling or a special understanding. This dwelling glory prefaced and foreshadowed the indwelling presence of God's Holy Spirit in our lives today. That special gift was first given to the Jewish people.

The covenants

God made promises throughout the Old Testament. These were always tied to a covenant. Be that covenant with Adam, Noah, Abraham, Isaac, or Jacob, or the covenant with Moses establishing the law, the priesthood, or the nation, or the covenant with David, the promises of God were always bound up in covenant. Sometimes those covenants were conditional. God made promises of blessings contingent on the other party's acceptance of the terms. Sometimes those promises were eternal and unconditional. One of those unconditional promises was in the Abrahamic covenant found in Genesis 12 and 15. God promises the land of Israel to Abraham and his descendants without stipulation.

We live now under a new covenant, but that covenant does not simply do away with the older covenants. In fact, in the Bible every successive covenant was built on the foundation of the previous covenant. Ultimately they all point back toward the promise of God in the Garden of Eden and then to the covenant with Abraham, and they point toward the sanctifying and redemptive work of Jesus as the means of our salvation.

The law

The very bedrock of human government is the law of God. Government can try as hard they like to strip away the Ten Commandments from the public square, but Paul aptly points out in Romans 2:15 that "the law [is] written in [our] hearts, [our] conscience also bearing witness."

Yes, the law of God is written on our hearts, but the written law came through the Jewish people. Once codified, it was no longer up for interpretation. Hardened human hearts could not vainly seek out evil and call it good with impunity. That precious written Word, more than just the Ten Commandments, which David called "a lamp to my feet and a light to my path" (Ps. 119:105), entered this world at the prompting of the Holy Spirit, and through the careful preservation of Jewish scribes, it has endured the ages.

While we do not live under the Law of Moses insofar as the sacrificial system as a means of our salvation or right standing with God, we do observe the law as a divine standard. The law points out our shortcomings and our need for a Savior.

Service

Along with the law, this sacrificial system pointed out not only the depth and breadth of man's sin but also the sheer impossibility of performing enough works to redeem ourselves. In this the sacrificial system points to Christ as the coming once-and-perfect sacrifice who would not only provide redemption and atonement but who would also perfectly fulfill the image foreshadowed within the sacrificial system.

There are five basic types of offerings mentioned in the Old Testament: the burnt offering, the grain offering, the peace offering, the sin offering, and the trespass offering. In the context of each offering, there were three distinct participants: the priest, the offering, and the offeror. Each sacrifice had particular instructions as to what could and could not be offered, what the particular offering was for, and who (God, priest, or offeror) was to receive which portion of the offering.

When mingled together, these offerings collectively give us a view of Christ. No one sacrifice could adequately represent the awesomeness of His coming and sacrifice. Indeed, within the perfect sacrifice of Christ, Jesus occupied the place of priest, offering, and offeror, for no priest could be higher, no offering more perfect, and no offeror more pure of heart. In Ezekiel 45:17 we read, "He must provide the sacrifice for sin, the oblation, the burnt offerings and the communion sacrifices to make expiation for the House of Israel" (NJB). And so Jesus did.

Promises

In mentioning the covenants earlier, I talked about promises God made. While the covenants were almost always made with specific people, the promises were always for "you and your descendants" (Gen. 17:7). The Jewish people were the first inheritors of God's promises. Among these were that they would be "a great nation," that they would receive perpetual ownership of all the land from Egypt to the Euphrates, and that they would be God's "special possession" and a kingdom of priests and a holy nation.

Most importantly present among these promises was the hope of a coming Messiah and a better day wherein God Himself would rule as King over Israel. These promises, among others, have held together Jewish identity through trials, tribulation, persecution, and pain.

Christ

Two of the Gospels take great pains to establish the lineage of Christ. Matthew traces the lineage of Jesus from Abraham forward, while Luke traces the lineage of Jesus back all the way to Adam. It is interesting to note that Matthew, who wrote his Gospel with a focus toward the Jewish people and emphasizing the role of Jesus as Messiah, was careful to include not just the Jewish members of

Jesus's family tree but also the Gentiles (Ruth and Rahab) and the prostitutes (Tamar and Rahab, again). I will expound on this later.

What is significant is that Jesus's genealogy reads like a "Who's Who" of the Jewish people. Present in the line are Abraham, Isaac, and Jacob, of course, but also Judah, Boaz, King David, Solomon, and Josiah. Forty-two generations from Abraham to Jesus are packed with a plethora of notable figures. Jesus was Jewish to His core!

The great privilege was not only that the Messiah came *through* them but also that Messiah came *to* them. The apostle John in his Gospel says that Jesus "came to His own," but, unimaginably, "His own did not receive Him" (John 1:11). This is why we read in Romans 11:3–7 that the Jewish people sinned against God and ultimately refused these privileges.

The Unimaginable Burden

In Romans 11:1 Paul writes inspiring words of comfort when he says, "I say then, has God cast away His people? Certainly not!" But there are stipulations and limits to that statement. However, as we continue in Romans 11, Paul goes on to write what are, in my opinion, some of the saddest words in the entirety of Scripture. In verses 7–8 he wrote:

> What then? Israel has not obtained what it seeks; but the elect have obtained it, and the rest were blinded. Just as it is written: "God has given them a spirit of stupor, eyes that they should not see and ears that they should not hear, to this very day."

The centuries of waiting and poring over the Torah, all the Rabbinic commentaries, and the commentaries on the commentaries looking for clues about their precious Messiah were lost on them. "They have not obtained what they seek," says Paul, but others have obtained it in their stead. Paul even quotes the words of Moses, their treasured law-giver, and David, their most precious earthly king, when he says that they had received "eyes to see and ears to hear, to this very day" (Deut. 29:4) and their table became "a snare and a trap, a stumbling block and a recompense to them" (Rom. 11:9; see also Ps. 69:22).

In these verses we see a nation blinded. Except for a small elect group they are blind and deaf, burdened because of their rejection of Messiah. They are in darkness to the gospel.

Even this is God's sovereign purpose. Don't dare believe those who say that the church has somehow replaced the Jewish people or that the Jews are beyond hope. Paul continues on and says two remarkably important things in Romans 11. Paul says, "I say then, have they stumbled that they should fall? Certainly not!" Hallelujah! God does not leave His chosen ones without hope.

But there is an even more somber affirmation Paul makes. He tells us that not only will the Jews not fall away completely but also that "through their fall, to provoke them to jealousy, salvation has come to the Gentiles. Now if their fall is riches for the world, and their failure riches for the Gentiles, how much more their fullness!" (Rom. 11:11–12). Yes, you read that right! Their rejection is the means of the world's reconciliation. Their poverty bestows riches on the entire world. Not only does the church have the Jews to thank for salvation, but also, according to Paul as prompted by the Holy Spirit, their stumbling benefits the entire world, and because of that, their ultimate reward will be great!

Until

For the most part, in its early history and even today, the Jews have stood alone. The children of Abraham have survived captivities, persecutions, and holocausts from Assyrians, Babylonians, Romans, Nazis, and Communists. All have at one time or another sought their extinction, but the Jews survive as a testimony to God's power. I ask as did Twain, "What is the secret of the Jews' immortality?"

God is the reason. God promised their preservation. In Jeremiah 31:34–37 the prophet declares God's word to the people:

No more shall every man teach his neighbor, and every man his brother, saying, "Know the LORD," for they all shall know Me, from the least of them to the greatest of them, says the LORD. For I will forgive their iniquity, and their sin I will remember no more.

Thus says the LORD, who gives the sun for a light by day, the ordinances of the moon and the stars for a light by night, who disturbs the sea, and its waves roar (The LORD of hosts is His name):

"If those ordinances depart from before Me, says the LORD, then the seed of Israel shall also cease from being a nation before Me forever."

Thus says the LORD:

"If heaven above can be measured, and the foundations of the earth searched out beneath, I will also cast off all the seed of Israel for all that they have done, says the LORD."

God says that the only way for the Jews to cease being not only a nation but also His chosen people is if the sun goes dim, the stars fade, the ocean waves no longer billow, the heavens become measureable, and the earth be literally burned away. Such is His devotion to His chosen. God's love for Israel is an everlasting love.

When the Arabs attacked the Jews in 1948, Secretary of State George Marshall said, "Within ten maximum fifteen days, not a single Jew will be alive in Palestine."[6] Then in 1967 Egypt, Jordan, Syria, Iraq, Saudi Arabia, Morocco, Algeria, Libya, Tunisia, Sudan, and members of the PLO and the Arab Expeditionary Forces attacked the Jewish state. In only six short days Jews, who were outnumbered ten to one, won the war. Israel lost about 759 soldiers in that war, while the opposing armies lost approximately 17,000.[7] In 1973 Egypt attacked Israel across the Sinai Peninsula, and by the end of the conflict, the IDF (Israel Defense Forces) had advanced to within sixty miles of Cairo!

THE FUTURE HOPE

I have stayed for the most part in Romans 11 for this chapter, because rightly understanding those passages in Paul's letter to the Roman church is critical in understanding God's economy of salvation with regard to not only the Jew but also the Gentile as well. There is much in that little chapter to cause consternation and even scoffing, but embrace the truth of Paul's words. If you do, you can reach verse 25. Paul explicitly states that we should not be ignorant of the mystery, lest we be wise in our own opinions. For "blindness in part has happened to Israel until the fullness of the Gentiles has come in." That word *until* is so beautiful. There is a blindness now, and it will remain until a certain thing is accomplished: the fullness of the Gentiles. This is not the place to consider this mysterious phrase. But what is important is the very next phrase penned by Paul: he speaks of the blindness remaining only until the "fullness of the Gentiles" comes in, and then he says in verse 26, "And so all Israel will be saved."

This will happen during the end times. The scales will fall from the Jews' eyes after the Rapture, and in the midst of that great and final holocaust, Israel shall receive her Messiah. Zechariah 12:9–14:20 describes that day: In that terrible day Jesus will set foot on the Mount of Olives and cleave it asunder, creating a new valley in Israel. Night will be like day. Jesus will utterly destroy the nations that attack Jerusalem, and after that He will pour out on the house of David and all the inhabitants of Jerusalem a spirit of grace and supplication. They will look on Him, the One they pierced, and they will mourn for Him as one mourns for an only child. They will look on Him and ask, "What are these wounds on Your body?" And Jesus will reply, "These wounds I received in the house of My friends." (See Jeremiah 13:6.) They will see Him for who He is, and they will worship.

The valley of dry bones shall come to life as a vast gospel army to witness to the world. The opposing nations shall be completely destroyed. And then all nations shall be judged according to how they treated Israel. (See Matthew 25.) Yes, the children of Abraham will survive it all to welcome back Jesus as the Bridegroom of the church and the Messiah of Israel.

The Mystery Revealed

This chapter has what would be in a movie a twist ending. I will not ask you to do it now, but go through this chapter again, and every time you see the word *Israel*, replace it with the word *you*. You see, if you are in Christ, all of those promises apply to you. If you are in Christ, all of the blessings apply to you. Let me summarize.

Just as God did not choose Israel because of anything they had done right, so it is with you. You have not earned God's love by your righteousness, nor can you. Further, you cannot through stiff-necked stubbornness lose God's love. He sets it on you for the sake of His Son.

In the same way that God did not give Israel the Promised Land when they were on the banks of the Jordan but instead promised it to them before they were even born by pledging it to their father Abraham, so has His promise of a heavenly home been yours since before the earth was formed. Because of your acceptance of Christ, you have become an heir with Abraham. How?

Because you are God's by *adoption*! Read that section again and realize how inextricably God has brought you into His family! Because of that, you have received the dwelling *glory* of God, the precious Holy Spirit. Because of that, you are now a partaker of the promises of His *covenants*. This change makes you able to love His law and to mimic the attitude of the *service* shown to you by making yourself a living sacrifice so that you can receive not only the *promises* of the past but also those of the future as well. And, like the Gentiles and harlots who were in the lineage of *Christ*, you have been embraced by God. You do not have to hide who you are, for God has made you a new creation.

The mystery of Israel's survival is not just that they have survived but that their survival is a living picture that in Christ you will live and not die. Your life is meaningful and full of purpose. God made you, chose you, and loved you from the foundation of the world, and no amount of persecution, tribulation, or trial will snatch you from His hand. In Christ you are a child of the King— princes and princesses, royal priests and heirs to all that God has to give you. Don't forfeit your privileges!

Chapter 20

The MYSTERY *of* INIQUITY
and the ANTICHRIST

ARK DAVID CHAPMAN had worshipped John Lennon
for fifteen years. It is almost inexplicable, then, that on
December 8, 1980, mere hours after asking Lennon for
an autograph, Chapman stood outside The Dakota building and
fired his .38 revolver five times, hitting Lennon with four hollow-
point bullets in the back. Shortly after the murder Lennon's little
boy Sean asked why the man killed his daddy.

In December 2008 the body of two-year-old Caylee Anthony
was found a quarter of a mile from her Orlando, Florida, home.[1]
She had been reported missing by her grandmother.[2] The chief suspect in the case, her mother, Casey Anthony, was found not guilty
after a six-week trial.[3] Still, the world is left to wonder, what happened? Who could have done that to little Caylee, and, more importantly, why?

The crowd had gathered there near Tucson, Arizona, at the
Safeway store to meet US Representative Gabrielle Giffords.
Suddenly blasts cut through the blather as a gunman, Jared Lee
Loughner, opened fire. Spectators subdued Loughner, but the
chilling deed had been done. Among the dead were federal judge
John Roll and nine-year old Christina-Taylor Green. Loughner's
intended target, Representative Giffords, had sustained a massive
injury to the head after being shot at point-blank range.[4]

Iranian President Mahmoud Ahmadinejad said in a Piers
Morgan interview, "I'm in love with all of humanity."[5] But this is

the same man who said, "Thanks to people's wishes and God's will, the trend for the existence of the Zionist regime is [headed] downwards, and this is what God has promised and what all nations want. Just as the Soviet Union was wiped out and today does not exist, so will the Zionist regime soon be wiped out."[6] Additionally, while being interviewed by ABC's Christiane Amanpour, he unequivocally lied about the sentencing of Sakineh Ashtiani, saying that a stoning sentence had never been issued.[7] As the political leader of Iran, the responsibility of the treatment of the Iranian citizen stops at his desk, and yet citing Iran's human rights violations would take volumes.

In China and Tibet during the years between 1949 and 1969, Chairman Mao Zedong had over seventy-five million of his fellow citizens killed.[8] Hitler was responsible not just for the deaths of Jews but also of other civilians during World War II, to the amount of twelve million souls.[9] Leopold II of Belgium had eight million citizens of the Congo killed.[10] Joseph Stalin killed over six million Russian citizens during the time of the gulags and the manipulated famine.[11] Pol Pot of Cambodia etched almost two million people onto his body count.[12] Slobodan Milosevic killed one hundred thousand citizens of Yugoslavia.[13]

Why? Not only these crimes but also countless others raise the same perplexing questions. News reports every day list a litany of incomprehensible atrocities, and we are left to wonder, "Why?" A world left to its own devices has no answer. The atheist, the humanist, the relativist, nor the pragmatist can answer this question. They are left to call "evil" a "sickness" and somehow turn the perpetrator into a victim, thus effectively sweeping under the rug the entire problem.

Paul called this issue the mystery of evil (2 Thess. 2:7). Evil is a mystery. Its origins have been questioned throughout recorded history. Evil is birthed out of sin. It began when Lucifer uttered his first "I will" (Isa. 14:13–14), and it spread from his lips into the hearts of humanity. Still, we are left with, "Why?" Evil is still a mystery.

It is mysterious in its deceitfulness. Over and over again people follow the same path to sin. How often do we hear the convicted criminal or even the recovering addict say, "I thought I could handle it." Music artist Carlos Whittaker tells the story of meeting a man who had come to his current town to start his life over. Two years prior the man had molested his ten-year-old stepdaughter. Whittaker says that the fifty-six-year-old man told him that his sin had escalated from pornography to prostitutes to molestation in just two years.

Evil is mysterious in its destructiveness. How many MADD commercials and anti-drinking and anti-drug PSAs aired during the last few decades? And yet every night there are tales of people being arrested for DUI or, worse, killing themselves or others because of the influence of alcohol and drugs.

Evil is mysterious in its devastation. Even in light of all of these tales, mankind cannot seem to stop sinning. We are just as wicked today as we have ever been despite our so-called progress. We have program after program to combat drugs, alcohol, poverty, illegitimacy, and every kind of evil, but they all fail. James said that "each one [of us] is tempted when he is drawn away by his own desires and enticed. Then, when desire has conceived, it gives birth to sin; and sin, when it is full-grown, brings forth death" (James 1:14–15).

In light of the fact that they cannot provide solutions to the problems, modern thinkers have simply renamed sins so that man will not feel so guilty. A drunkard now has the disease of alcoholism. An adulterer can easily be labeled a sex addict, and so we are expected to feel sorry for the culprit rather than those hurt by the infidelity, and we gently rename the act an affair. Stealing the life savings of your customers is called "misappropriating funds." Political spin that is an obvious lie results in the liar being saddled with a "credibility gap." A pedophile can be nearly exculpated from his crimes when we discover that he too was molested as a child. Even a stone-cold murderer can blame his acts on the consumption of too much junk food, and we point accusing fingers at Twinkies and soda.

Man can decorate sin with new names, but the vile results still show. Efforts to deny sin are futile, and yet we still make the attempt. Why do we do this? It is an awful mystery.

THESSALONICA

We live in this sin-cursed world. The just suffer with the unjust (or, more appropriately worded, the *justified* suffer with the unjust). Why is that? Is it fair? There is an entire branch of theology called "theodicy" that addresses those, and similar, questions. I am not addressing those here. What I want to focus on is not the problem of evil but the existence of it, mankind's fascination with and inability to escape it.

In his second known letter to the church at Thessalonica Paul wrote of a coming period of iniquity that would make previous eras of sin pale in comparison. The works of Mao, Hitler, Stalin, and the like will seem like timorous steps into evil by comparison. This period would be couched in a time near the return of Jesus Christ. Paul wrote:

> Now, brethren, concerning the coming of our Lord Jesus Christ and our gathering together to Him, we ask you, not to be soon shaken in mind or troubled, either by spirit or by word or by letter, as if from us, as though the day of Christ had come. Let no one deceive you by any means; for that Day will not come unless *the falling away* comes first, and the *man of sin is revealed*, the son of perdition, who opposes and exalts himself above all that is called God or that is worshiped, so that *he sits as God in the temple of God*, showing himself that he is God.
>
> Do you not remember that when I was still with you I told you these things? And now you know what is restraining, that he may be revealed in his own time. For the *mystery of*

lawlessness is already at work; only He who now restrains will do so until He is taken out of the way. And then *the lawless one will be revealed*, whom the Lord will consume with the breath of His mouth and destroy with the brightness of His coming. The coming of the lawless one is according to the working of Satan, with all power, signs, and lying wonders, and with all unrighteous deception among those who perish, because they did not receive the love of the truth, that they might be saved.

—2 Thessalonians 2:1–10, emphases added

Many scoff at the very idea of this kind of person. That a man could rise up in such a way to control so much of the known world and yet be so evil, they say, is the stuff of fairy tales. When they say this, I point them to two world leaders: Adolf Hitler and Barack Obama.

Now before I proceed let me say this: I do not in any way believe that Barack Obama is the Antichrist, nor do I compare him politically or socially to Hitler. It is *only* their rise to power that I focus on here.

In the early twentieth century one of the strongest republics in the world, even more so than that of the United States, was that of Germany, called the Weimar Republic. A financial crisis hit, and the value of their currency, the *reichsmark*, plunged. In 1919 a lowly corporal who had no formal education and no career prospects, hoping to stay in the army as long as possible, accepted an assignment to infiltrate the German Workers' Party (DAP). While there he adopted founder Anton Drexler's anti-Semitic, nationalist ideology. He began speaking in local beer halls, and his natural charisma and speaking ability gained him legions of admirers. In less than two years Hitler assumed leadership of renamed National Socialist German Workers' party (NSDAP). It was at this point that he assumed the title "der Fuehrer." After serving two prison sentences, one for disrupting a government meeting and the other for attempting to overthrow the German government, he was released from prison and began his proper political ascent. By 1932 he was elected chancellor of Germany. In less than two decades Adolf Hitler went from being an uneducated soldier with no prospects, clinging to life in the army, to being one of the most powerful men on the planet.

Rising from relative obscurity, lawyer and community organizer Barack Obama was elected to one of the state senate seats for Illinois in 1996. In 1999 he ran for Congress, but poor state congressional attendance and other issues led to his defeat. In 2004 Obama won the Illinois primary for a shot at the national Senate seat. His opponent Jack Ryan, in an onslaught of sex scandals, quit the race. Obama would eventually win against the Republican replacement candidate, Alan Keyes.

It was his speech at the 2004 Democratic National Convention that thrust then Senator Obama into the international spotlight. His charisma and speaking ability captivated those in attendance. I remember sitting in my living room watching the convention and hearing his speech, and I thought to myself, "There is no way that man won't be president one day." Outside of Illinois his name was hardly known, but after the DNC convention the name Barack Obama was on the lips of every politico in the nation. This was 2004.

Barely two short years later Senator Obama announced his campaign for presidency. His election was considered by many to be a lock from the start. His speeches enthralled the crowds at every whistle stop and rally he attended. In November 2008, four short years after his landmark speech at the DNC, Obama won the presidential election, scoring 52.9 percent of the vote, beating his opponent, John McCain, by almost ten million popular votes and landsliding the electoral college vote by almost two hundred more votes than his opponent. In his election for a second term President Obama was reelected in yet another landslide!

This happened in less than a decade. These two men are not the only examples, but they are, in my opinion, the starkest examples.

On paper neither candidate had the requirements or experience to reach their position, but they did reach it, and they did it quickly. So when people say to me that a man cannot rise from obscurity into a position of power in the way described by Paul, I point to the pages of history and say, "It has already happened."

So the possibility of the man is there. But what else did Paul say would happen?

The church at Thessalonica suffered under the onslaught of wickedness. Times were so bad that some had begun wondering if they had missed the return of Jesus. They were, according to Paul, shaken and troubled. The word that Paul uses is actually a nautical term that means to be knocked loose from anchor. The stormy winds of sin blow until the anchor of faith is loosened. The word *troubles* means terrified! Understand the state of the Christians at Thessalonica. They were so afraid that they had begun to lose their faith. How like us today! I admit, I sometimes look around at the sin running rampant and that is even endorsed in our country and in the world, and I am tempted to question God's love for us. "How can You love us?" I wonder.

Evil and suffering are rampant in our world. It shakes us and terrifies us. Sin seems to be out of control. All over the world the wicked prosper and the innocent suffer. We look for a reason and find nothing but a mystery.

The Antichrist

But Paul tells us that one day the source, the very origin of iniquity, will be revealed. One day all the hidden things of darkness, all the vileness of evil, will be placed in one person. That man, the Antichrist, will reign in this world and will be loved like no leader before him. He will promise peace but bring destruction. He will promise prosperity but bring poverty. More than this, he will make and then dreadfully break a covenant with Israel. He will go into the rebuilt temple and seat himself as God over the earth.

When will this happen? Paul tells us clearly that this will only occur after we are gathered to Jesus in the Rapture (2 Thess. 2:1), after a great apostasy (v. 3), and after the Jewish temple is rebuilt (v. 4). We have discussed the Rapture. What is this "apostasy" or falling away?

Apostasy is often translated as a falling away from faith, and that is a perfectly acceptable definition. However, the word Paul uses here is like a military term that means not an abandonment of one's post but a reassignment of one's post. So what Paul says is that the "lawless man" will not be revealed until we have been reposted! He reaffirms twice for the Thessalonians and for us that if the church is here, we have nothing to fear from the son of perdition, because he has not been revealed yet. And why? Because for him to be revealed, we have to be reassigned to our heavenly home!

But make no mistake, the man will come. Just as God sent His Son, Satan will send his son, the son of perdition. He will be the embodiment of all that is wicked and evil. The term *wicked* is the Greek word *lawless*. It means unprincipled. "Son of perdition" is the same phrase used of Judas in John 17:12. The son of perdition stands against all that God stands for. He will exalt himself to be God.

However, for now evil is being restrained. Though restrained, evil is still present, and the same spirit that will fill and control the Antichrist is already working. And why is it restrained? It is hindered by the presence of the church. The only thing that keeps sin from completely overrunning the world is the church. We are the light that keeps the world from being completely engulfed in darkness. We are the city of refuge (see Numbers 35:6–28) for the hopeless sinner.

First John 4:1–3 declares that Antichrist is to come, but the evil forces are at work now. If you have immoral principles, you are a "lawless one." If you stand against what God stands for, you are in the spirit of antichrist. If you refuse to bow before God, you are in league with Satan. The Bible says, "Woe to those who call evil good, and good evil; who put darkness for light, and light for darkness;

who put bitter for sweet, and sweet for bitter!" (Isa. 5:20). Still, when the Antichrist is revealed, it will eventually become clear that his power, though supernatural, is sinister at its source.

The Mystery Revealed

The revelation of the evil one will be overshadowed by the revelation of Jesus Christ. Verse 8 of 2 Thessalonians 2 says that the Lord will consume the Antichrist with "the breath of His mouth" and will destroy the son of perdition with "the brightness of His coming." Yes, evil operates today, but in Christ we are protected from the fear of evil, because "greater is he that is in [us], than he that is in the world" (1 John 4:4, KJV). With Christ in us, we can not only recognize evil for what it is, but with the Holy Spirit in us, we can also root it out of our lives. Praise God for victory over the mystery of evil!

Chapter 21

The MYSTERY *of the* ETERNAL WORLD

SOME DAYS I feel old. Recently I had a fairly major cardiac event, and I made drastic lifestyle changes. My health has dramatically improved, and most days I feel as if my life has just started. But there are still some days when I just feel old. I feel simultaneously that I have lived for so long but done so little and have so much left to do. I have seen in my lifetime the explosion of television and home computing; I have seen computers go from being the size of a large house to being small enough to fit in my pocket: I carry in my hand a tablet device that holds multiple translations of the Bible, volumes of Bible commentaries, dictionaries, lexicons, great works of theology from heroes of the faith, my complete contacts list, access to e-mail, the Internet, and even VoIP phone, as well as my favorite video games. It takes up less space than the old marbleized composition journals of my college years. I feel as if I have lived a long time.

Yet my life span is nothing when compared to eternity. You see, we often become obsessed with lifespan and death and how long is too long or too short for a person to live, but what we have forgotten—yes, one of the greatest long cons ever pulled by Satan—is that we were not meant for this world. No, this fallen, corrupted planet is a shell of what it once was, a bitter mockery of its former glory and perfection. We were never meant to live short lives on a tarnished earth.

But it is to the grave we will go. No matter how much we fight or travail, death comes. And as Emily Dickinson said, if we do not stop for death, death will kindly stop for us. These things are inevitable, they say: death and taxes.

But is that true?

Living and Dying

Long before the Book of Genesis was written, the Book of Job was penned. Job posed a question for the ages when he queried, "If a man dies, shall he live again?" (Job 14:14). Hundreds of years later Jesus would answer that question at the tomb of His friend Lazarus. He said, "I am the resurrection and the life. He who believes in Me, though he may die, he shall live. And whoever lives and believes in Me shall never die" (John 11:25–26).

Jesus declared that a day would come when the dead bodies of all who believe in Him would be resurrected. This, of course, is the time of the Rapture, which we have discussed previously. However, it bears repeating that part of the inheritance of the believer at the time of the Rapture is a new body. That new body is a blessing, but it is also a requirement. Heaven and eternity do not exist in the same dimension in which we currently exist, and the flesh-and-blood bodies you and I currently have cannot exist in that heavenly dimension.

Additionally Jesus alludes to a generation that would be alive on the earth at the time of this resurrection and that would not die. This is supported in 1 Corinthians 15:51 where Paul writes, "Behold, I tell you a mystery: We shall not all sleep, but we shall all be changed." This will happen at the speed of light. It is often said that it will happen "in the twinkling of an eye," but what the phrase in 1 Corinthians 15:52 actually means is "faster than you can blink your eye." We often think of a blink as something that is very fast, and it is. It takes approximately .4 seconds for a human eye to fully blink. But did you know that a ninety-five-mile-per-hour fastball travels from the pitcher's hand to the catcher's mitt in .395 seconds? That is faster than a blinking eye. And the phrase used here is yet faster than that. It is the word that indicates the flash of lightning. This is 186,000 miles per second!

At that time we will embrace our God-intended state and put off our mortal coil for immortality (1 Cor. 15:53), and death will be no more (vv. 54–55)! We have become far too accepting of death. Now I do not think that a funeral needs to be either an overly somber event or a hyper-jubilant event. Death should be understood in its proper context. While we rejoice that a Christian goes on to be with the Lord, there should be a part of us that is angry—not because a loved one has been taken away, but the focus of our anger should be upon our enemy the devil! He brought death into this world.

Order out of chaos

We do live in turbulent times, and I do believe that the end is near. I have taught many times, as have others, that there exists no condition yet unmet for the Rapture to happen. We wait patiently on the Lord while doing the work He has set for us to do, but we are not to be ignorant of the facts regarding this time in history.

Those who have died are not "gone." They have not ceased to exist. They are alive and conscious in the other realm. The greatest example to accommodate understanding of this that I have ever heard is this:

> Assume you are in your car, and you are driving down the road. Everything is going great. The windows are down, the wind is blowing, the sun is shining, and the radio is blasting. Suddenly the engine starts to make a little noise. Pings and knocks reverberate through the interior. The gas pedal is working only intermittently. You check the fuel gauge. There is plenty of fuel. Suddenly lights start flashing, steam starts pouring, oil is spraying, and you ease the car over to the side of the road. The engine stops. You turn the keys in the ignition, but the starter only spins, until eventually it gives up altogether and makes no more noise at all. Your car is dead.

> When you get out of your car…do you cease to exist? That's all death is. It's the real you, getting out of a dead car.

At the moment of death the believer's spirit receives a temporary covering and is conscious in Jesus's presence. The Holy Spirit in us is our guarantee of our place in that other realm.

HEAVEN

There is a great misconception about many Christian preachers. I have heard people say that they just did not understand how preachers could be so happy about people going to hell. Let me assure you right now that for me this is not the case, and for any whom it is so, I can assure you that they do not represent the teachings of Jesus. Scripture says that God is not willing that any should perish but that every person would accept eternal life (2 Pet. 3:9).

Still, all through Scripture we are made aware that all humans will live forever, either in God's presence in heaven or separated from God in hell. Daniel spoke in a prophetic warning:

> And many of those who sleep in the dust of the earth shall awake, some to everlasting life, some to shame and everlasting contempt. Those who are wise shall shine like the brightness of the firmament, and those who turn many to righteousness like the stars forever and ever.
>
> —DANIEL 12:2–3

The truth of this passage is sobering enough, but look at what is, I think, the most important word: *everlasting*. Daniel said that some of the dead would rise to life and some to contempt but that both states would be everlasting.

Many theories have arisen to try to water down or even debunk this truth. Some have said that God will not condemn people to hell forever but that He will annihilate them from existence. Others have said that God will, at some point in eternity future, redeem those consigned to hell. This idea is called universalism or universal reconciliation. A form of this idea was recently touted in Rob Bell's book *Love Wins.*

These ideas sound good, and they certainly warm the heart, but they do not agree with Scripture. Scripture is clear about salvation. Jesus said, "I am the way, the truth, and the life. No one comes to the Father except through Me" (John 14:6). In response to the question "What must I do to be saved?" the apostle Paul said, "Believe on the Lord Jesus Christ, and you will be saved, you and your household" (Acts 16:31). Later, in the Book of Hebrews, we read that physical death is a great line in the sand. In Hebrews 9:27 we read, "It is appointed for men to die once, but after this the judgment." All of this coalesces perfectly with the picture painted by Daniel.

The good news is that for the believer, Jesus promised heaven, and not just some pie in the sky heaven but a real place where He was going to prepare a special home for each one of us (John 14:1–6). So what is it?

Ultimately heaven is being present with the Lord (2 Cor. 5:8), but we must understand that heaven exists in a different dimension from our current reality. Second Corinthians 4:17–18 says:

> For our light affliction, which is but for a moment, is working for us a far more exceeding and eternal weight of glory, while we do not look at the things which are seen, but at the things which are not seen. For the things which are seen are temporary, but the things which are not seen are eternal.

One of the greatest lies perpetrated on the lost is that this world, this reality, is all that there is or even that it is the ultimate experience. No! There are realms we cannot begin to see or understand, and they are everlasting! The things we can see—this world, sickness and infirmities, crime, loss, and despair—are all temporary! The things we cannot see, that dimension beyond which our corporeal senses are able to engage, is a place where all that is temporary is removed forever!

There will be no sickness. There will be no grief or despair. There will be no aching bones or muscles. There will be no failure. There will be no crime or ill intent. There will be no loss, because "to die is gain" (Phil. 1:21)!

The very concept of time is erased in eternity. There is no yesterday or tomorrow in eternity; there is only now. There is no "old" in heaven. Revelation 21:1–5 says:

> Now I saw a new heaven and a new earth, for the first heaven and the first earth had passed away. Also there was no more sea. Then I, John, saw the holy city, New Jerusalem, coming down out of heaven from God, prepared as a bride adorned for her husband. And I heard a loud voice from heaven saying, "Behold, the tabernacle of God is with men, and He will dwell with them, and they shall be His people. God Himself will be with them and be their God. And God will wipe away every tear from their eyes; there shall be no more death, nor sorrow, nor crying. There shall be no more pain, for the former things have passed away."
>
> Then He who sat on the throne said, "Behold, I make all things new." And He said to me, "Write, for these words are true and faithful."

Look at that word *new*. Jesus tells John, "I make all things new." This is so fascinating. This is the Greek word *kainos*. It means "new," but it doesn't mean "new" in the way we use it in English. To help you understand the enormity of this, I will have to use a couple of illustrations.

A young pastor I know jokes about how he has a weakness for food. Not food in general, mind you. He has a weakness for *new* food. If his favorite restaurant is promoting a new dish, he cannot help himself but to order it, even if he wants his usual. If his favorite beverage has a new flavor, he tells me he has to try it. There is something, he says, about the newness of the experience.

I love to work. I love to be doing. Sleep for me is a break between doing things. But I love sleep. What I really love is coming in to a perfectly made bed with high-thread-count sheets, a memory-foam mattress, and pillows; the cool of the bedding lulls me into sleep. Inevitably, however, the spot I lie in gets warm. I have to flip the pillow and adjust myself until I am in such a deep sleep that the warmth does not distract me.

I love talking to new first-time parents. The wonder of their situation is beautiful to behold. I have stood in rooms with young couples when their child is brought in for the first time, and I have watched tears of pure joy flow down their faces.

I give you these examples, insubstantial shadows though they are, to try to convey what Jesus meant when He said He makes all things new. First of all, He used the word *make*. That is a present tense verb. In Greek this verb is present active indicative. Now hold that thought.

The word *new*, I have already said, is *kainos*. What this word means is "new" in the sense of "fresh" or "unused." I have touched on this word in other books, but for our purposes here let's look at what these two words when put together in Greek mean.

In the eternity of heaven Jesus will cause everything to be in a current, right-now state of refreshed newness. With regard to my illustrations, imagine if every bite of every kind of food tasted as if it was your first bite of food *ever*; imagine lying down after an exhausting day to a bed that was so perfectly new that the sheets never warmed, and when you woke refreshed and stood up from the bed, you turned around and saw a perfectly made bed waiting for your return; imagine an encounter not just with loved ones, friends, and saints you have read about, or perhaps never even heard of, but with the God who gave everything to make your reunion with Him possible; imagine seeing Jesus for the first time, and then imagine every second of eternity feeling as you did that very first time. In eternity Jesus makes all things new!

The traveling city

There will be a new heaven and a new earth, but Jesus will rule from Jerusalem; it is just not the Jerusalem we know now. John the beloved apostle saw this city and measured it. In Revelation 21:10–21 we read:

> And he carried me away in the Spirit to a great and high mountain, and showed me the great city, the holy Jerusalem, descending out of heaven from God, having the glory of God. Her light was like a most precious stone, like a jasper stone, clear as crystal. Also she had a great and high wall with twelve gates, and twelve angels at the gates, and names written on them, which are the names of the twelve tribes of the children of Israel: three gates on the east, three gates on the north, three gates on the south, and three gates on the west.
>
> Now the wall of the city had twelve foundations, and on them were the names of the twelve apostles of the Lamb. And he who talked with me had a gold reed to measure the city, its gates, and its wall. The city is laid out as a square; its length is as great as its breadth. And he measured the city with the reed: twelve thousand furlongs. Its length, breadth, and height are equal. Then he measured its wall: one hundred and forty-four cubits, according to the measure of a man, that is, of an angel. The construction of its wall was of jasper; and the city was pure gold, like clear glass. The foundations of the wall of the city were adorned with all kinds of precious stones: the first foundation was jasper, the second sapphire, the third chalcedony, the fourth emerald, the fifth sardonyx, the sixth sardius, the seventh chrysolite, the eighth beryl, the ninth topaz, the tenth chrysoprase, the eleventh jacinth, and the twelfth amethyst. The twelve gates were twelve pearls: each individual gate was of one pearl. And the street of the city was pure gold, like transparent glass.

It is difficult to conceive of this city without a physical comparison. We do not make cities like this anymore, but imagine a fortress, a walled city. The city of God is foursquare, and each side is approximately 1,500 miles long. Now get this picture for comparison: the outline of the city of God in Revelation measures from the Eastern seaboard of the United States to Colorado and from the Canadian border to the southern tip of Florida. That makes the area of the city 2,250,000 square miles.

But we also read that the height of the city is equal to its width and breadth. The city is as high as it is wide. Either in cube or pyramid shape, this city is enormous. If a cube, then the city is 3,375,000,000 cubic miles. And listen to this: given this size, it can house 100,000,000 people, giving each of them 2,000 square feet to call their own. And that's just the city from which Jesus will rule!

HELL

I have said it before, but it bears saying again: it is never pleasant to talk about hell. I never enjoy talking about hell. But that's me. What is more important is that God despises the very idea of any of His creation going into hell. Hell is a place that God created out of necessity. It is a place created specifically for "the devil and his angels" (Matt. 25:41) and not for man.

So why do I say that there are those among us now and who have been here who will find themselves in the "everlasting contempt" (Dan. 12:2) of Daniel's prophecy? Because it does not matter what I think or say; it matters what Jesus said, and Jesus taught that hell was a literal place where people would go if they did not accept Him as the Son of God and as their Savior.

Jesus was desperate for people to miss hell. Listen to the dramatic statements He made in Mark 9:43–48:

> If your hand causes you to sin, cut it off. It is better for you to enter into life maimed, rather than having two hands, to go to hell, into the fire that shall never be quenched—where "Their worm does not die and the fire is not quenched."
>
> And if your foot causes you to sin, cut it off. It is better for

you to enter life lame, rather than having two feet, to be cast into hell, into the fire that shall never be quenched—where "Their worm does not die, and the fire is not quenched."

And if your eye causes you to sin, pluck it out. It is better for you to enter the kingdom of God with one eye, rather than having two eyes, to be cast into hell fire—where "Their worm does not die and the fire is not quenched."

Consider the enormity of that! Your eye is causing you to sin? "Pluck it out," says Jesus. It would be better to be blind, physically deformed, and challenged than to allow your intact body to lead you into hell.

We need to be careful about hell. The general assumption about hell is that it is a place ruled by Satan, who commands his minions to torture those whom God has consigned there; it is a place of fire and burning flesh, and those who go there will linger in a fire that never consumes, while being stabbed with pitchforks for the duration of eternity.

Friends, this is not hell.

Let's look at some of the various places in Scripture where hell is described. In the above verses (Mark 9) Jesus used the word *Gehenna* for "hell." This was a valley outside the city of Jerusalem. It was where babies were burned in ovens in offerings to Baal. By Jesus's day it had become the city dump. Now do not imagine a city dump in the kind of civilized way we know it today. The rotting corpses of criminals were tossed into Gehenna, and wild dogs were known to come and eat at their flesh. Maggots were constantly found in the refuse, and fires were continually burning throughout the valley.

Now when Jesus spoke of Gehenna, he was not saying that the Valley of Gehenna was the place where the impenitent are relegated for eternity. Rather, Jesus chose the most vivid, disgusting example He could find to explain to us that hell was a place to be avoided.

So what is hell? This is a hard question to answer, because to understand it, we have to first grasp what hell is not.

Every day when you wake up, you are a recipient of God's prevenient grace. That simply means that God shows love to you, even if you are unconverted, in many of the same ways He shows love to His faithful children. You receive the benefit of sunshine, cool breezes, rain, the fruit of the land; you miraculously escape a car accident, or perhaps you find favor in some other way. The point is, God showers His love on you, and you benefit from the presence of the Holy Spirit every day that you live life. God uses this grace to gently draw the unrepentant to Him.

In hell all of that goes away. Forever. The reason Jesus used such graphic imagery for hell is because we could never grasp the implications if He had said, "Hell is having none of God's presence or grace." We hear that, and it seems like nothing. But it is the most unimaginable horror of that state. Imagine never smiling—not because you have nothing to smile about (you won't) but because you are incapable of feeling joy. Imagine never laughing again—not because you have nothing to laugh about (you won't) but because you have lost the ability to laugh. Imagine never again feeling the urge to sing, dance, spin, wonder, imagine, create, be in relationship, or connect with another human *ever again*! Imagine remembering but not being remembered. Try to imagine, if you can, never again saying "Thank God" for anything (even if you only say it flippantly now)—not because you have nothing for which to be thankful (you won't) but because the concept of gratitude is lost to you.

That is hell.

The torment of hell is not fire and brimstone, pitchforks and claws, or, as Dante supposed, aimless wandering, unsatisfied lust, icy rain, foul swamps, or any kind of eternal violence. Hell is a place utterly without God.

The inevitable response

I have shared this with people before, and I hear the same thing from them every time. "That's not fair," they protest. "To have no proof of God here, and then to die and see that hell is real, only not to be able to make the choice then, is just wrong." Just as frequently I hear, "I can't believe there is a loving God who would send people to hell for all eternity just because they chose not to submit."

Let me be clear here: God will "send" only the devil and his angels to hell. Every other person who makes hell his eternal home will do so because he rejected God's grace and love.

In Ezekiel 18:25–32 God addressed this attitude in the people of Israel:

> "Yet you say, 'The way of the Lord is not fair.' Hear now, O house of Israel, is it not My way which is fair, and your ways which are not fair? When a righteous man turns away from his righteousness, commits iniquity, and dies in it, it is because of the iniquity which he has done that he dies. Again, when a wicked man turns away from the wickedness which he committed, and does what is lawful and right, he preserves himself alive. Because he considers and turns away from all the transgressions which he committed, he shall surely live; he shall not die. Yet the house of Israel says, 'The way of the Lord is not fair.' O house of Israel, is it not My ways which are fair, and your ways which are not fair?
>
> "Therefore I will judge you, O house of Israel, every one according to his ways," says the Lord God. "Repent, and turn from all your transgressions, so that iniquity will not be your ruin. Cast away from you all the transgressions which you have committed, and get yourselves a new heart and a new spirit. For why should you die, O house of Israel? For I have no pleasure in the death of one who dies," says the Lord God. "Therefore turn and live!"

That is what God says to you, to me, to all of us. Our ways, our plans, our ideas, our thoughts are flawed, and they lead to destruction. But the God of the universe says, "Turn and live!"

THE MYSTERY REVEALED

Simply put, every person who has ever been born is, from the moment of their conception (and even before the foundation of the world, really), destined for eternity. It is our rightful place. It is our God-intended home. But God gave us a will to choose, and He will never infringe on that freedom. If we choose to accept Him, then the wonder and beauty of heaven, the New Jerusalem, the new heaven, and the new earth await us. If we choose to reject Him, He has prepared a place where we can go that honors our wishes and every horrible implication thereof.

Second, every person who has ever been born is, in the words of Nuno Bettencourt and Gary Cherone, "Hole Hearted." There is a piece missing in us. We try to fill it with success, money, relationships, hobbies, work, food, drugs, sex, and anything else our hearts can devise, but the only way for us to be complete is to be reconciled to our Creator.

God does not wish that any of us perish, but His holiness, His justice, demands that our wishes be respected. If we accept the sacrifice of His precious Son, Jesus, then we will spend eternity with Him. If we reject Jesus and choose to go our own way, we will spend eternity completely absent from Him.

Jesus made it clear in Revelation 21:8 that some would not enter into eternity with Him when He said:

> But the cowardly, unbelieving, abominable, murderers, sexually immoral, sorcerers, idolaters, and all liars shall have their part in the lake which burns with fire and brimstone, which is the second death.

But for those who accept the sacrifice and lordship of Jesus, He said:

> Behold, the tabernacle of God is with men, and He will dwell with them, and they shall be His people. God Himself will be with them and be their God. And God will wipe away every tear from their eyes; there shall be no more death, nor sorrow, nor crying. There shall be no more pain, for the former things have passed away.
> —Revelation 21:3–4

There is an eternity to spend somewhere. You are destined for it. You are made for heaven and not for hell, but your eternal destiny is decided by your earthly decisions. Choose Jesus! Turn and live!

Epilogue

The MYSTERY *of* GOD FINISHED

I N REVELATION 10:7 John tells us that "the mystery of God would be finished." This announcement takes place "in the days of the sounding of the seventh trumpet." Clearly this "sounding" goes on for an extended time. Remember in Revelation that there are three terrible cycles of judgment: the seven seals are opened, and then the seventh seal begins the seven trumpet judgments. The seven trumpet judgments signals the final seven bowls of wrath to be poured out. (See Revelation 6–16.)

This announcement will signal the awful truth that the delay of God's ultimate judgment on sin, Satan, and every human system is over. Revelation 10:6 says, "And [the angel] swore by Him who lives forever and ever, who created heaven and the things that are in it, the earth and the things that are in it, and the sea and the things that are in it, that there should be delay no longer." God has postponed the final judgments out of mercy toward humanity. That long season of mercy will have come to an end.

The seventh trumpet heralds the final surge of God's wrath on evil! In previous chapters we have discussed the "mystery of iniquity" that has been at work on earth since the fall of Satan and since Adam's fall in the garden. The awful effects of evil form a dark underbelly in human history. The earth is a vast graveyard that bears the mark of Satan's design and many evils. The "days of the sounding of the seventh angel" (Rev. 10:7) are days that signal large movements in heaven and upon the earth. Jesus will take possession of the earth at His return to reign. (See Revelation 19:11.)

In those days all the hidden things will be revealed! In context it would seem that Satan, sin, the Antichrist, the false prophet, human government, man-made religion, the economic system, and human wisdom will be utterly cast down. All of these systems will be exposed for their failure, inadequacy, and folly! When we read from Revelation 10 through Revelation 22, we realize that all wickedness will be overthrown by Jesus.

This epic moment will announce the imminent return of Jesus to the earth and the final transfer of all authority on earth to His sovereign reign. In Jesus's reign evil will be vanquished, Satan and the Antichrist overthrown, the Jewish people will be restored, the economy will collapse, the final campaign of Armageddon will be carried out, and Jesus Christ will descend back to the earth. At His coming Jesus will have on a robe that declares Him "King of kings and Lord of lords" (Rev. 19:16).

In John 19:30 Jesus declared, "It is finished!" This was a prophetic saying indicating that the cross had released the word that would bring an end to Satan, death, and evil! Revelation 10:7 heralds the mighty fulfillment of what Calvary wrought for us. Hebrews 4:3 declares that "his work has been finished since the creation of the world" (NIV). At long last the mystery has been revealed and finished!

The finished mystery not only announces the end of evil's reign, but it also heralds the enthronement of the Lord Jesus Christ soon to happen on earth (Rev. 11:15–19). In Revelation 10:6–7 the delay will be over, and then all mysteries will be revealed. A redeemed humanity will have fullness of knowledge. Now we only "know in part" (1 Cor. 13:9–10). The mystery revealed is that there is coming a glorious day in which the work will be over and there will be no more mystery.

In that day we will see the undoing of Satan's plan and the restoration of humanity to God's ancient intent! The wonderful truth is no longer a secret. Human beings can be whole and live a joyful and deathless eternity:

It may be at morn when the day is awaking
When sunlight through darkness and shadow is breaking...
It may be at midday, it may be at twilight
It may be perchance that the blackness of midnight
Will burst into light in the blaze of His glory
When Jesus receives "His own."[1]

Jesus's greatest desire is to spend eternity with you and to reveal every mystery to you.

BIBLIOGRAPHY

Antonacci, Mark. *The Resurrection of the Shroud: New Scientific, Medical, and Archeological Evidence.* New York: M. Evans & Co., 2000.

Banks, William D. *The Heavens Declare.* Kirkwood, MO: Impact, 1985.

Blum, Howard. *The Gold of Exodus: The Discovery of the True Mount Sinai.* New York: Simon & Schuster, 1998.

Bucklin, Robert. "An Autopsy on the Man of the Shroud." 2007. http://shroud.com/bucklin.htm (accessed May 23, 2013).

Castleden, Rodney. *Atlantis Destroyed.* New York: Routledge, 2001.

Dake, Finis J., Mark Allison, and David Patton. *Another Time, Another Place, Another Man: A Biblical Alternative to the Traditional View of Creation.* Lawrenceville, GA: Dake Publishing, 1997.

Feinberg, Charles Lee. *Israel at the Center of History & Revelation.* Portland, OR: Multnomah Press, 1980.

Fisk, Robert. "The United States of Israel?" *Counterpunch*, April 27, 2006. http://www.counterpunch.org/2006/04/27/the-united -states-of-israel/ (accessed May 23, 2013).

Fleming, John. *The Fallen Angels and the Heroes of Mythology.* Dublin: Hodges, Foster, & Figgis, 1879.

Foster, Karen Polinger, Robert K. Ritner, and Benjamin R. Foster. "Texts, Storms, and the Thera Eruption." *Journal of Near Eastern Studies* 55, no. 1 (1996): 1–14.

Graham, Billy. *Angels: God's Secret Agents.* Garden City, NY: Doubleday, 1975.

Greene, Brian. *The Elegant Universe: Superstrings, Hidden Dimensions, and the Quest for the Ultimate Theory.* New York: W. W. Norton & Company, Inc., 1999.

Horn, Thomas R. *Nephilim Stargates: The Year 2012 and the Return of the Watchers.* Crane, MO: Anomalos Publishing, 2007.

Hutchings, Noah, Bob Glaze, and Larry Spargimino. *Marginal Mysteries: A Biblical Perspective.* Crane, MO: Defender, 2012.

Jones, Brandon. "Mona Eltahawy, Egyptian Born MSNBC Pundit, Arrested for Vandalizing Pro-Israel Poster." *The Global Dispatch*, September 27, 2012. http://www.theglobaldispatch.com/mona-eltahawy-egyptian-born-msnbc-pundit-arrested-for-vandalizing-pro-israel-poster-video-24309/ (accessed May 23, 2013).

Josephus, Flavius. *The Works of Josephus: Complete and Unabridged.* Translated by William Whiston. Peabody, MA: Hendrickson, 1987.

Kilkenny, Niall. "The United States of Israel." 2010. http://www.reformation.org/united-states-of-israel-pdf.html (accessed May 23, 2013).

Larkin, Clarence. *Dispensational Truth, or, God's Plan and Purpose in the Ages.* Philadelphia: Rev. Clarence Larkin Estate, 1920.

Masefield, John. *The Trial of Jesus.* New York: The MacMillan Company, 1925.

Mavor, James W. *Voyage to Atlantis: The Discovery of a Legendary Land.* New York: Putnam, 1969.

Mills, Philo Laos. *Prehistoric Religion: A Study in Pre-Christian Antiquity.* Washington: Capital Publishers, Inc., 1918.

Montgomery, John Warwick. *History & Christianity.* Downers Grove, IL: InterVarsity Press, 1971.

Morison, Frank. *Who Moved the Stone?* New York: The Century Co., 1930.

Pember, G. H. *Earth's Earliest Ages and Their Connection with Modern Spiritualism and Theosophy.* New York; Chicago: Fleming H. Revell Co., 1900.

Philo. *The Works of Philo: Complete and Unabridged.* Translated by Charles Duke Yonge. Peabody, MA: Hendrickson, 1993.

Quintilianus, Marcus Fabius. *The Lesser Declamations 1.* Cambridge, MA: Harvard University Press, 2006.

The Book of Jasher. Eastbourne, England: Gardners, 2010.

The Ugly Truth. "The United States of Israel" (video). http://theuglytruth.wordpress.com/2011/03/30/the-united-states-of-israel/ (accessed May 23, 2013).

Thomas, W. H. Griffith. "Proofs of the Resurrection." *Moody Bible Institute Monthly* 22, no. 1, September 1921.

NOTES

Chapter 2
The Mystery of the Days of Noah

1. G. H. Pember, *Earth's Earliest Ages* (Whitefish, MT: Kessinger Publishing, 2003). Viewed at Google Books.

2. Ibid.

3. Flavius Josephus, *The Works of Josephus: Complete and Unabridged*, trans. William Whiston (Peabody, MA: Hendrickson, 1987).

4. Philo Judaeus, *The Works of Philo: Complete and Unabridged*, trans. Charles Duke Younge (Peabody, MA: Hendrickson, 1993).

5. Charles Deloach, *Giants* (Lanham, MD: Scarecrow Press, 1995).

6. Mohamed Cherif, *The Giants* (n.p., TheBookEdition, n.d.).

7. Wikipedia, "Homo heidelbergensis," http://en.wikipedia.org/wiki/Homo_heidelbergensis (accessed May 20, 2013).

8. Ted Twietmeyer, "Evidence of Giants Who Walked the Earth," http://rense.com/general79/giants.htm (accessed May 20, 2013).

9. United States Census Bureau, "World Population: 1950–2050," http://www.census.gov/population/international/data/idb/worldpopgraph.php (accessed May 20, 2013).

10. United Nations, Department of Economic and Social Affairs, "World Population Prospects, the 2010 Revision," http://esa.un.org/wpp/Analytical-Figures/htm/fig_1.htm (accessed May 20, 2013).

11. MooresLaw.org, "Moore's Law," http://www.mooreslaw.org/ (accessed May 20, 2013).

Chapter 3
The Mystery of the Great Pyramid

1. Auguste Mariette, *The Monuments of Upper Egypt* (N.p.: A. Mourès, 1877).

2. Greatpyramid.org, "The Great Pyramid," http://greatpyramid.org/aip/gr-pyr1.htm (accessed May 20, 2013).

3. National Geographic, "Great Pyramid," http://www.nationalgeographic.com/pyramids/khufu.html (accessed May 20, 2013).

4. Greatpyramid.org, "The Great Pyramid."

5. World-Mysteries.com, "Mystic Places—The Great Pyramid," http://www.world-mysteries.com/mpl_2.htm (accessed May 20, 2013).

6. Greatpyramid.org, "The Great Pyramid."

7. Patrick Heron, *The Nephilim and Pyramid of Apocalypse* (New York: Kensington Publishing Group, 2004).

8. The Great Pyramid, http://www.europa.com/~edge/pyramid.html (accessed June 14, 2013).

9. Theodore Spencer Case and Warren Watson, eds., *The Kansas City Review of Science and Industry* (Kansas City, MO: Ramsey, Millett & Hudson, 1879). Viewed at Google Books.

10. J. Bernard Nicklin, *Testimony in Stone* (Merrimac, MA: Destiny, 1961) 17.

11. Gizapyramid.com, "An Arab Who Got the Shock of His Life on the Summit," http://www.gizapyramid.com/gip2.htm (accessed May 20, 2013).

12. Merrill F. Unger, *The New Unger's Bible Dictionary* (Chicago: Moody Publishers, 2006).

Chapter 4
The Mystery of Sodom and Gomorrah

1. Wyatt Archeological Research, "Cities of the Plain," http://www.wyattmuseum.com/cities-of-the-plain.htm (accessed May 20, 2013).

2. Flavius Josephus, *The Life and Works of Flavius Josephus*, trans. William Whiston (Whitefish, MT: Kessinger Publishing, 2006).

Chapter 5
The Mystery of Melchizedek

1. *The Book of Jasher* (Eastbourne, England: Gardners, 2010).

Chapter 6
The Mystery of Lost Atlantis

1. Wikipedia.org, "Uniformitarianism," http://en.wikipedia.org/wiki/Uniformitarianism (accessed May 21, 2013).

2. Lawrence Durrell, *The Greek Islands* (London: Faber & Faber, 2002) in Kathleen Burke, "Archeology and Relaxation in Santorini," *Smithsonian.com*, July 28, 2011, http://www.smithsonianmag.com/travel/europe-asia-pacific/Archaeology-and-Relaxation-in-Santorini.html (accessed May 21, 2013).

3. Rodney Castleden, *Atlantis Destroyed* (New York: Routledge, 2001), 117.

4. Charles Pellegrino, *Unearthing Atlantis* (New York: Random House, 1991), 13-27.

5. Ibid.

6. Ibid.

7. Karen Polinger Foster, Robert K. Ritner, and Benjamin R. Foster, "Texts, Storms, and the Thera Eruption," *Journal of Near Eastern Studies* 55, no. 1 (1996): 1–14.

Chapter 7
The Mystery of the Angels

1. Francis Brown, S. Drive, and C. Briggs, *Brown-Driver-Briggs Hebrew and English Lexicon* (n.p. Hendrickson Publishers, 1996).
2. Billy Graham, *Angels: God's Secret Agents* (Garden City, NY: Doubleday and Company, Inc., 1975, 1995), 30.

Chapter 8
The Mystery of Mount Sinai

1. For more information see Howard Blum, *The Gold of Exodus: The Discovery of the True Mount Sinai* (New York: Simon & Schuster, 1998).

Chapter 9
The Mystery of the Lost Ark of the Covenant

1. This term *father* here means "ancestor"; it also shows Josiah's authority as king and the similarities of his and David's hearts after God. Josiah's reign is actually sixteen generations down the ancestral line from David.
2. Wyatt Archeological Research, "The Ark of the Covenant," http://www.wyattmuseum.com/arkofthecovenant.htm (accessed May 21, 2013).
3. Marcus Fabius Quintilianus, *The Lesser Declamations 1* (Cambridge, MA : Harvard University Press, 2006).
4. Wyatt Archeological Research, "The Ark of the Covenant Special Article," http://www.wyattmuseum.com/ark_of_the_covenant_special.htm (accessed May 21, 2013).
5. Ibid.
6. Ibid.
7. Ibid.
8. Ibid.

Chapter 11
The Mystery of Hanukkah

1. About.com, "What Is Hanukkah?", http://judaism.about.com/od/holidays/a/hanukkah.htm (accessed May 22, 2013).

Chapter 12

The Mystery of Christ

1. Livingway.org, "The Matchless Pearl," http://livingtheway.org/pearl.html. Used by permission.

Chapter 13
The Mystery of the Magi

1. As quoted in Roger Highfield, *The Physics of Christmas* (New York: Hachette Book Group, 1998). Viewed at Google Books.

Chapter 14
The Mystery of the Empty Tomb

1. This was quoted by an unnamed Garden Tomb official to the author in the course of one of twenty-two trips to Israel. Also quoted in John J. Rousseau and Rami Arav, *Jesus and His World* (Minneapolis, MN: Augsburg Fortress, 1995). Viewed at Google Books.

2. Holy Land Voyager, "The Garden Tomb," http://www
.tourstotheholyland.com/christian-travel-guide/christian-sites/the-garden
-tomb.aspx (accessed May 22, 2013).

3. W. H. Griffith Thomas, "Proofs of the Resurrection," *Moody Bible Institute Monthly* 22, no. 1, (September 1921).

4. Frank Morison, *Who Moved the Stone?* (New York: The Century Co., 1930).

5. As quoted in John Stott, *Basic Christianity* (Grand Rapids, MI: Wm. B. Eerdmans Publishing, 1958).

6. John Masefield, *The Trial of Jesus* (New York: The MacMillan Company, 1925).

7. John Warwick Montgomery, *History & Christianity* (Downers Grove, IL: InterVarsity Press, 1971), 78.

8. As told in W. A. Criswell, *Why I Preach That the Bible Is Literally True* (Nashville: Broadman & Holman, 2000), 167.

Chapter 15
The Mystery of the Shroud of Turin

1. Britannica.com, "Shroud of Turin," http://www.britannica.com/
EBchecked/topic/609725/Shroud-of-Turin (accesed May 22, 2013).

2. Wikipedia.org, http://en.wikipedia.org/wiki/Radiocarbon_14_dating_
of_the_Shroud_of_Turin

3. Harry E. Grove, *Relic, Icon or Hoax?* (Bristol, UK: Institute of Physics Publishing, 1996).

4. TheHolyShroud.net, "Where Was the Shroud From 1204 to 1357?",
http://www.theholyshroud.net/KnightsTemplar.htm (accessed May 22, 2013).

5. Ibid.

6. TheHolyShroud.net, "History of the Shroud," http://www
.theholyshroud.net/History.htm (accessed June 20, 2013).

7. PBS.org, "Case File: Shroud of Christ?", http://www.pbs.org/wnet/secrets/previous_seasons/case_shroudchrist/ (accessed June 20, 2013).

8. Shroud.com, "Shroud History," http://www.shroud.com/history.htm (accessed June 20, 2013).

9. TheHolyShroud.net, "History of the Shroud."

10. Mark Guscin, "The Sudarium of Oviedo: Its History and Relationship to the Shroud of Turin," http://www.shroud.com/guscin.htm (accessed May 23, 2013).

11. Robert Bucklin, "An Autopsy on the Man of the Shroud," http://shroud.com/bucklin.htm (accessed May 22, 2013).

12. Ibid.

13. Ibid.

14. Ibid.

15. Ibid.

16. Ibid.

17. Ibid.

18. Victor Volland, "Floral Images on Shroud of Turin Intrigue Botanist—He Believes Plants Prove Cloth Dates from Time of Jesus," *St. Louis Post-Dispatch,* June 8, 1997, http://www.questia.com/library/1P2-33075091/floral-images-on-shroud-of-turin-intrigue-botanist (accessed May 22, 2013).

19. Shroud2000.com, "Evidence From Pollen and Flower Images," http://shroud2000.com/ArticlesPapers/Article-PollenEvidence.html (accessed May 22, 2013).

20. Mark Antonacci, *The Resurrection of the Shroud* (New York: M. Evans and Company, Inc., 2000).

21. Ibid.

22. Mark Antonacci and Arthur Lind, "Particle Radiation From the Body" Resurrection of the Shroud Foundation, https://docs.google.com/document/d/19tGkwrdg6cu5mH-RmlKxHv5KPMOL49qEU8MLGL6ojHU/edit?hl=en_US (accessed May 23, 2013).

23. Ibid.

24. Ibid.

25. Ibid

26. Antonacci, *The Resurrection of the Shroud.*

27. Ibid.

Chapter 16
The Mystery of the Church

1. Story told in a sermon by the late Stephen Olfu at an Alabama Evangelism Conference in 1981 in Birmingham, Alabama.

Chapter 19
The Mystery of Israel's Survival

1. Reprinted in *Mark Twain, Collected Tales, Sketches, Speeches and Essays: 1891–1910* (New York: Library of America, 1992).

2. Ibid.

3. Robert Fisk, "The United States of Israel?" *Counterpunch*, April 27, 2006, http://www.counterpunch.org/2006/04/27/the-united-states-of-israel (accessed May 22, 2013); *The Ugly Truth*, "The Unites States of Israel" (video clip), March 30, 2011, http://theuglytruth.wordpress.com/2011/03/30/the -united-states-of-israel (accessed August 4, 2012); Niall Kilkenny, "The United States of Israel," 2010, http://www.reformation.org/united-states-of -israel-pdf.html (accessed May 22, 2013).

4. Brandon Jones, "Mona Eltahawy, Egyptian-Born MSNBC Pundit, Arrested for Vandalizing Pro-Israel Poster," *The Global Dispatch*, September 27, 2012, http://www.theglobaldispatch.com/mona-eltahawy-egyptian-born -msnbc-pundit-arrested-for-vandalizing-pro-israel-poster-video-24309 (accessed May 22, 2013).

5. Fadi Eyadat, "Survey Finds Nearly Half of Israeli Arabs Deny Holo- caust," http://www.haaretz.com/print-edition/news/survey-finds-nearly-half -of-israeli-arabs-deny-holocaust-1.276206 (accessed May 22, 2013).

6. As quoted on Lasthour.com, "Israel, the 20th Century Miracle," http:// www.lasthour.com/miracle_of_Israel.htm (accessed June 14, 2013).

7. Israel Ministry of Foreign Affairs, "The Six-Day War Introduction," http://www.mfa.gov.il/mfa/foreignpolicy/mfadocuments/yearbook1/pages/ the%20six-day%20war%20-%20introduction.aspx (accessed May 22, 2013).

Chapter 20
The Mystery of Iniquity and the Antichrist

1. Walter Pacheco, Sarah Lundy, and Amy L. Edwards, "Remains Iden- tified as Missing Toddler Caylee Anthony," *Orlando Sentinel*, December 19, 2008, http://www.orlandosentinel.com/news/local/breakingnews/orl-bk -caylee-anthony-body-dna-121908,0,1859200.story (accessed May 22, 2013).

2. Katie Escherich, "TIMELINE: Caylee Anthony Case Captivates Country," ABC News, July 5, 2011, http://abcnews.go.com/TheLaw/caylee -anthony-case-timeline-autopsy-released/story?id=6448060#.UZ36XNJzEZB (accessed May 23, 2013).

3. Jessica Hopper, Emily Friedman, and Aaron Katersky, "Casey Anthony Trial: Not Guilty Murder Verdict," http://abcnews.go.com/US/ casey_anthony_trial/casey-anthony-guilty-murder-caylees-death/story?id =13987918 (accessed May 22, 2013).

4. Devin Dwyer, Kevin Dolas, Dean Schabner, and Emily Friedman, "Cops Hunt Second Man Believed to Be Involved in Congresswoman Giffords Shooting," ABC News, January 8, 2011, http://abcnews.go.com/ Politics/rep-gabrielle-giffords-shot-grocery-store-event/story?id=12571452# .UZ38i9JzEZA (accessed May 23, 2013).

5. Piers Morgan Tonight, "Interview With President Mahmoud Ahmadinejad," September 24, 2012, http://transcripts.cnn.com/TRANSCRIPTS/ 1209/24/pmt.01.html (accessed May 23, 2013).

6. *Haaretz*, "Ahmadinejad at Holocaust Conference: Israel Will 'Soon Be Wiped Out,' December 12, 2006, http://www.haaretz.com/news/ ahmadinejad-at-holocaust-conference-israel-will-soon-bewiped-out-1 .206977 (accessed May 23, 2013).

7. International Campaign for Human Rights in Iran, "Stand Up to Ahmadinejad's Falsehoods," September 20, 2010, http://www .iranhumanrights.org/2010/09/ahmadinejad-lies/ (accessed May 23, 2013).

8. Piero Scaruffi, "The Worst Genocides of the 20th and 21st Centuries," http://www.scaruffi.com/politics/dictat.html (accessed May 23, 2013).

9. Ibid.

10. Ibid.

11. Daryna Krasnolutska and Halia Pavliva, "Ukraine Irks Russia With Push to Mark Stalin Famine as Genocide," Bloomberg.com, January 3, 2008, http://www.bloomberg.com/apps/news?pid=newsarchive&sid=akRdu1cuBP Kg&refer=europe (accessed May 23, 2013).

12. Scaruffi, "The Worst Genocides of the 20th and 21st Centuries."

13. Ibid.

Epilogue
The Mystery of God Finished

1. "Christ Returneth" by H. L. Turner. Public domain.